The Art of Writing Music

The Art of Writing Music

A practical book for composers and arrangers of instrumental, choral and electronic music as applied to publication, films, television, recordings and schools.

JOHN CACAVAS

With a special chapter on Electronic Music by Steve Kaplan

Alfred Publishing Co., Inc., Los Angeles

Published by Alfred Publishing Co., Inc.

16380 Roscoe Blvd., Van Nuys, Calif. 91406

Copyright © 1993 by Alfred Publishing Co., Inc.

Printed in the United States of America

Library of Congress Cataloging in Publication Data

Cacavas, John.
    The art of writing music : a practical book for composers and arrangers of instrumental, choral, and electronic music as applied to publication, films, television, recordings, and schools / by John Cacavas; special electronic section by Steve Kaplan.
       p.   cm.
    ISBN 0-88284-618-3. — ISBN 0-88284-619-1 (pbk.)
    1. Composition (Music) I. Kaplan, Steve. II. Title.
MT40.C12 1993
781.3—dc20

93-2594
CIP
MN

Item No.: Softcover 4163

           Hardcover 4161

Project Editor: Dave Black

CONTENTS

CONTENTS

ABOUT THE AUTHOR

John Cacavas is one of the most prolific and influential composers of his generation, having published over 2,000 works, many of which have been recorded. His compositions and arrangements are performed in concert halls around the world, and his work for stage, television and film has made him one of the busiest and most sought-after composers in the entertainment industry.

Born in Aberdeen, South Dakota, he attended Northern State University where he established his musical skills throughout his college years. He directed a dance band at Northern and later transferred to Northwestern University where he produced an NBC radio program spotlighting original works by student and faculty composers. After he graduated from Northwestern University with a degree in composition and theory, he joined the armed forces where he served as an arranger with the United States Army Band in Washington, D.C.

Cacavas' unique comprehension of the relationship between visual media and music has enabled him to score over 600 one-hour TV shows and 70 television movies including "Kojak," *The Executioner's Song*, "Columbo," "Hawaii Five-O," "Matlock," "The Equalizer" and "Murder She Wrote." He has scored 15 feature films including *Airport '75* and *Airport '77* and special sequences from *The Hindenburg* and Martin Scorsese's *King of Comedy*.

His awards include two Freedoms Foundation Awards, two Emmy nominations and a Grammy award for *Gallant Men*, an album he made in 1968. He lives in Beverly Hills with his wife, Bonnie Becker, a writer.

PREFACE

MUSIC! Even the word sounds wonderful. Mysterious and exotic. *Harmony. . . coloratura. . . soprano. . . violin. . .* they all sound melodious to the ear. The word *melody*, too, flows and is pleasing when spoken. *Counterpoint. . .* well, that's a little suspect. Maybe too cerebral. *Fugue* is a little harsh too, but there are more than enough words to make my point.

Whether their origins are Greek or Italian, the words that make up the various facets of music send a signal to the brain of something pleasurable, romantic and, to the non-musician, mysterious and sometimes baffling.

And what *is* music? A certain thing that happens to the voice box that shifts gears and results in singing, usually pleasurable. People sawing with bows, blowing through pipes and horns, striking keys and hitting things.

These productions of sounds we define as music have been with us for a long time. Progress improved the capabilities of the instruments, and a few new ones have been added along the way, but basically not much has changed. At one time or another, various people have sat down and written out the components of the symphony orchestra. In its ordinary form it contains three trumpets, three trombones, four horns, woodwinds by twos, strings and percussion. Within the last century or so, we have added extra woodwinds, and other instruments such as harp, tuba and piano.

But all these players sitting on a stage would be useless without something to play. We would hear tuning up, perhaps a few well-known folk songs played willy-nilly, but nothing else. In other words, unless there is someone who is willing to sit down with pen and paper and create, the symphony orchestra, choir and band would be totally worthless.

What it comes down to is the fact that if there were no composers, there would be no music. On the other hand, if there were no musical organizations, the composer would never hear his or her music played, either. And then there is the conductor. Ah! Quite often it is the conductor who decides what the orchestra will play. Everybody is at his or her mercy. And of course, the conductor quite often is beholden to the person or board responsible for the hiring. So, in the final analysis, it often comes down to money and business, just like everything else. It may be art to some, but to others it's the old *do-re-mi*.

In spite of the dichotomy of art and business, music has flourished. We have been blessed with masterpieces of opera, symphony and ballet as well as small works. We have had a worldwide legacy of folk, pop and theater music, because of the people who have written the music and the words that sometimes accompany it. And it is also because of the people who have arranged or orchestrated this music. Although composition and orchestration are synonymous with serious composition, it is not the case with many other areas such as popular music and the music of the theater. In those cases, songs are written and later arranged. It also should be mentioned that to the vast majority of the public this craft of music arranging is all but unknown.

In the pages that follow, I hope to be able to contribute my experience along with the desire that I might make life a little easier for those of us who write music. It is not meant to be the definitive last word on the subject, nor is the intent to compete with the many other fine books that address these matters. The French have a word, *amusegueules*, which is a small morsel that precedes the first course at dinner. I hope you enjoy my little tidbit and get some satisfaction from it.

ACKNOWLEDGMENTS

It would be impossible for me to list everyone who has helped me in my musical career, but if it weren't for my parents, Harry and Barbara Cacavas, I might still be frying hamburgers somewhere. They encouraged me from the age of 13, even after I was booted out of piano class for lack of talent.

Next comes my beloved wife Bonnie, a great talent in her own right, psychiatric social worker, author, lyricist and wonderful mother.

To Morty and Iris Manus, the delightful owners of Alfred Publishing, I thank them for their support. Without their enthusiasm, there would be no book. Next, my personal thanks go to Dave Black and John O'Reilly of Alfred Publishing for their contributions, insight and hard work in making this book a reality.

I also want to thank the many producers and directors who gave me the chance to score their films, a debt that can never be repaid. I would like to list them in chronological order, spanning the beginning of my film career to the present:

Bill Frye, Telly Savalas, James McAdams, Matt Rapf, Irving Lerner, Harold Shampan, Ernie Pintoff, Burt Kennedy, Bert Leonard, Phil Yordan, Bernie Gordon, Joe Shaftel, Alan Gibson, Cy Chermak, Eugenio Martin, David Gerber, Roy Huggins, Howard Koch, Gary Nelson, Jack Smight, Richard Alan Simmons, Lawrence Schiller, Jay Daniel, S. Bryan Hickox, Fred Baum, Bud Austin, Nick Abdo, Bob Chenault, James Aubrey, Charles Sellier, Howard Avedis, Marlene Schmidt, Jerry Jameson, Bill McCutcheon, Jerry Isenburg, David Horwatt, Steve Cragg, Gary Nelson, Chris Chulak, Ken Johnson, Malcolm Stuart, Glen Larson, Alan Alda, Michael Economou, Delbert Mann, Roy Campenella Jr., Jon Epstein, Dean Hargrove, Mel Swope, Michael Scheff, Mary Anne Kasica, Todd London, Michele Burstin and E. Jack Neuman.

To the many publishers who have printed my music over the years:

the late Louis Dreyfus, Bonnie and Beebe Bourne, Arnold Brodio, Dean Burtch, Neil Kjos, Frank Connor, Chuck Barnhouse, Teddy Holmes, Jay Morgenstern, Martin Winkler, Ken Walker, Arthur Gurwitz, Harold Winkler, Sylvia Goldstein, Sol Reiner and, of course, Morty and Iris Manus.

To my film music agents:

Stan Milander, Jeff Kaufman, Kathy Schluessner, and Al Bart (now retired).

To my literary agent, Shirley Strick, an especially big thank you.

To Morton Gould, my indebtedness can never be repaid. He is a true artist and a wonderful person. It was through him that I really began to understand the mystery of music.

For each of us who has been lucky enough to make a living scoring films, he or she got their break in a variety of ways. In my case, a chance meeting with Telly Savalas in a London hotel opened the door: first, scoring some pictures in Europe, and then the call to Hollywood (as they say). If it wasn't for Telly's belief and confidence in me, I may never have gotten my break in Hollywood.

Telly Savalas is a consummate actor, gifted director, true friend and one of the most loyal human beings I have ever met. It is my pleasure and honor to dedicate this book to him.

John Cacavas
Beverly Hills, CA
March 1993

THE PROCESS

What is arranging? What is orchestration? These terms are bandied about interchangeably, but there is a difference between them. Loosely defined, the craft of orchestration involves transcribing music from a full sketch to a full score. In the motion picture business, an orchestrator works from anything from a three-line sketch to a complete condensed score of six or seven staves. In the case of John Williams and Morton Gould, for whom I have transcribed many scores for symphonic band, the sketch is complete down to the last dynamic indication. There is no arranging involved, except for the wind substitutions from strings. In the instances when I wrote the orchestrations for orchestra, all I did was simplify certain passages and perhaps eliminate the extreme high registers of the first violin.

An orchestrator does not introduce new patterns, countermelodies or the like. It is simply a literal transcription of the original intent. When one adapts a score to another medium (e.g., orchestra to band), it is still orchestration in the basic sense, assuming one is adhering to the original material. It is entirely possible to take an existing symphonic score and make an arrangement for concert band, such as one might do to make a very simple version of a difficult orchestral work. But it is unlikely that the writer would introduce new material into the original. So in this situation, it is still considered orchestration.

Arranging is a far more complex business and requires the additional skill of a composer. In its simplest context, it requires the arranger to work from a lead sheet and chord symbols only. It is up to the arranger to "cast" the work. He or she must decide who will play what, when and for how long. The arranger must devise modulations, backgrounds, counterpoint and harmonic substitution (on occasion) and be gifted enough to make it all sound right. Taking a song by Irving Berlin and arranging it for chamber orchestra is not orchestration but arranging, pure and simple.

Whether you are writing an arrangement or composing an instrumental work, starting out with a sketch has great advantages. First of all, it is written in concert pitch, which has obvious value. Second, in condensed form, it gives an overview of the entire piece's form, flow and so forth. And third, it makes it much easier to check harmonies and notes that might be suspect.

When you are ready to transfer your work to full score, you will have a second chance to look at it. You will be more familiar with your material and therefore able to see any shortcomings in a better light. There are countless changes I have made during this process, usually for the better.

In the area of film writing, the sketch is indispensable for timings, click-track beats, streamers and punches. Having twelve bars on a page to peruse is certainly better than the four bars you'll find on the average score page. I have been using a type of sketch paper that I first found at Universal Studios. It has a solid bar at the top (which I use mainly for tempos), measure numbers and synchronization nomenclature such as streamers. The paper can also be printed upside down, which allows the bar to act as a percussion staff. It can also be obtained in yellow or buff, but I've always preferred the white. I have found that the four staves work just fine, assuming I am going to orchestrate my own work. It would not be large enough for a substantial orchestra when someone else is going to do the orchestration.

You may also design your own sketch paper. There is an initial charge for making up the plate but if you do a lot of writing, it's worth it. An example of my paper is shown here. There are three systems on the page, which give me a total of twelve measures.

Sample Score Paper

PROD. _____ TITLE _____ REEL _____ PAGE _____

COMPOSER _____

One of America's greatest songwriters was Vernon Duke. He vacillated between writing serious music under his real name, Vladimir Dukelsky, and popular music under the nom de plume of Vernon Duke. Although his serious works are less well known, he wrote some of our greatest standards. Among them are "April in Paris," "Taking a Chance on Love," "Autumn in New York," "I Can't Get Started" and many others.

One evening we were entertaining him at a dinner party at our home in Connecticut, and at the request of our guests, I somewhat reluctantly asked him if he might play for us. After dinner, he was only too happy to oblige. We repaired to my studio, and the first request was "Autumn in New York."

He sat down, played a little intro and was on his way. When he got to the middle part, he stopped playing and looked at the keys for what seemed an eternity.

He shrugged, looked over at me and said, "I forgot the bridge."

Happens to the best of us.

RANGES AND KEY SELECTION

RANGES

Any composer or arranger who consistently forces players into the absolute top or bottom of their ranges is a fool (with the exception of keyboards or plucked instruments). The possibility of failing to hit the note always creates great apprehension in a player no matter how proficient he or she is. On exposed instruments the possibility becomes even deadlier, especially during solo passages.

Each instrument has its own limitations. The lowest note on a violin is G, and it is probably the easiest note to play. A saxophone's lowest note, however, is a low B-flat, and it is not easy to play. Extremely high notes for strings are weak and, for less-than-top-notch players, will probably be out of tune. Talk to instrumentalists and learn the strengths and weaknesses of their instruments.

A very funny story made the rounds of the Hollywood studio scene some time ago. At a film-scoring session at one of the major studios the producer asked the composer-conductor to have the violins play a certain passage one octave higher. The composer relayed this request to the violins.

–"I'm afraid we can't do that," said the concertmaster.

–"Why not?" asked the composer.

–"It's impossible; it'll take us out of range," replied the concertmaster.

–"Well, play it up a half-octave," answered the composer.

Sad, but true. As they say, it's not what you know but *who* you know in Tinsel Town.

Dynamics play an important part in the ranges that certain instruments can handle. A high C for a trumpet marked "pianissimo" is not only absurd but impossible to execute. Likewise, a low C on the flute marked "fortissimo" will elicit nothing but air. Common sense will lead you to the correct solutions in these areas. Again, if in doubt, just speak to the player.

I will refrain from including a range chart. Many are readily available and can be found in books on orchestration. Often in writing music for school publications, I provide optional notes for the first trumpets. If I cannot avoid a high note for the first clarinets, I divide them, with instructions for the top part to be played by one or two players.

If I am writing a unison part for four horns and the material is of a "soaring" nature, I might cue the third and fourth horns or give them something else to play. For school musicians, any high unisons for horns are dangerous. Although I hate to do it, I often cue the saxophones for these parts. The color is wrong, but one must play it safe with less mature players.

Even with top professional players the horn thing can be dicey. How often have you heard a "bubble" in the horns in a high passage during an orchestra or opera performance? It is just the nature of the instrument.

Oboes in unison? Very touchy. But what are you going to do when all the woodwinds are playing a passage in octave unisons? Leave the second oboe out? Cue it? I usually do the latter, although I suspect the second player could hold a grudge against me for my editorial decision. On the other hand, maybe I'll be thanked; who knows? In my experience, this problem with unisons has never involved any other wind players. Maybe somebody should reinvent the oboe.

When you are approaching the upper and lower ends of ranges during your writing you must ask yourself how it sounds. I know for a fact that although a trumpet can play a low G, it doesn't sound very good. There are certain instruments—the trombone, for example—that sound terrific in their extremes. The lowest notes are deep, biting and brassy. And if we remember Tommy Dorsey playing "I'm Getting Sentimental over You," we know how glorious the top notes can be. Just try to keep in mind whom you're writing for. French horns, also, have two separate registers. Up high, they are clear and soaring, and the lowest register is dark.

The lowest notes of the flute are useless, except when amplified. By this I mean that they don't carry, although they certainly sound good. In the professional area (mainly among studio musicians), the player may switch to either alto or bass flute, thereby ending the problems. No such luck with a high-school band, though.

The low notes of the alto saxophone are not that great for solo passages but are fine for section work. Just the opposite is true with the tenor and baritone saxophones. The baritone saxophone is especially thin in its upper register; the tenor saxophone less so.

Rangewise, the strings are the most versatile of all the instruments, with the exception of keyboards and certain mallet percussion instruments. The bottom note is defined, and the upper reaches depend on the ability of the player. As far as the registers are concerned, the colors vary from register to register. It really depends on the sound you are looking for. Again, if you are in doubt about a certain note on an instrument, just ask the player. Write it all down, memorize it and you'll be ahead of the game—the game being, in this case, making your music sound wonderful.

George Gershwin was a true bon vivant in every sense of the word. He was also a party animal and, with the slightest coaxing, would sit down at the piano and play all night long, usually with a beautiful young woman sharing his piano bench.

Of the fact that he was a ladies' man there was no question, although he never married. He died young, in his thirties, and either he never met the right one or he was having too much fun playing the field. If he had any women problems at all, it was probably keeping them away. After all, he was rich, famous, talented and, most of all, available. Now and then, however, he would meet someone who perhaps did not immediately succumb to his charms, and for that, he had a foolproof scheme.

He had written a song, a very pretty love ballad, and at the proper time, he would tell the young lady that he had written this song "just for you." Obviously, very few girls would not be impressed at the famous George Gershwin having written a song just for her. Unbeknownst to her, it was the same song for everyone. He just left the last note's lyric blank and filled it in with the name of his current heart's desire.

I asked his brother, Ira, if this story was true, and he said it was. "He got caught one time, though. He was dating a girl with a three-syllable first name, and she got suspicious when he tried to make the music fit. It was just a single note, you see."

I asked him, "Then what happened?"

"He just knocked off a couple of more tunes. One with a two-syllable ending, and one with three. That way he had everything covered."

I then asked him if the songs were any good. He thought a moment and said, "Not really. They weren't my lyrics, you see."

KEY SELECTION

Technically speaking, a piece of music can be composed in any key. The process of key selection only comes into play when you select the medium of orchestration. Strings tend to sound brighter in sharp keys, but then you have to consider the winds, which will then have multisharped keys. Brass instruments are more comfortable in flat keys (because of their construction), and woodwinds are somewhere in the middle.

Another consideration is the range of the melody. This becomes more apparent in choral arranging, where there are pretty much absolute limits. Although the range of an orchestra is much larger (because of the strings' registers), the practical range of a concert or jazz band will be much more limited.

The level of the performer's abilities must also be taken into consideration. If you write a string orchestra piece in D-flat, for example, you will have intonation problems. The same can be said about writing a concert band piece in the key of D major. With top-flight professional players, keys are less of a consideration because these performers can play anything.

Safe bets for school bands are the keys of F, B-flat, E-flat and, to a lesser degree, A-flat. For orchestra, the keys of C and F are probably the safest. For string orchestra, G and D are quite good.

Lots of music can be written without any key signatures at all. In my film music, I never use a signature unless it is an arrangement of a work that has a specific tonality. By not using a key signature and instead using accidentals throughout, I absolve the players from having to remember a signature. This works especially well in music of a constantly changing tonality. Psychologically it has other advantages, too. If, for example, you are forced into a section in the key of G with a young band, keep the signature the way it was (within reason, of course), and just use accidentals. If you indicate a lot of key changes with young players, you get a lot of problems.

This technique works well with young players. If you are in the key of E-flat and move to a section in A-flat, just add D-flats as you go along rather than change the signature. Again, the problem lies not so much in playing in the key of A-flat as it does in introducing another key signature.

Try to avoid signatures with many sharps or flats. You will then be faced with a lot of enharmonic spellings using double flats and sharps. It will be confusing for the players, and you will end up with needless mistakes in performance.

In writing arrangements for vocals, you will be locked into keys that will work with the singers' range. Most sheet music is printed in keys that suit the male singer. For the female "throat" voice, however, you will most likely have to move the key down at least a fourth. Sopranos, of course, will use the same key as the male singer.

Jazz bands will be more at home in the flat keys. Rock-and-roll groups with guitars, however, function better in the key of A or E (especially if they can't read music).

Really think about the key you are going to use and, even more important, about your modulations. Nothing is worse than to have written a whole piece (a full score, that is) only to find that you've picked a key that doesn't really work for one reason or another. Try to sketch your tops and bottoms out beforehand. It will save you time and trouble later.

> I was hired to conduct a CBS TV show in New York many years ago when doing it "live" was in vogue (by necessity, I gather). I was a little nervous because the orchestra was in one studio, the narrator in another and the ballet company was across town somewhere else. The score was written by a young lady who was fond of writing low B's for the piccolo, and low G-flats for the violins.
>
> It was a small orchestra, and the main purpose of the music was to underscore the narration and provide the accompaniment for the ballet. We were all ready to go; the director announced, "Stand by" and all of a sudden he said: "By the way, we're taking out the last half of the narration on the opening."
>
> I thought I was going to have a heart attack—or worse.
>
> There was no time to tell the orchestra anything, and then the red light went on.
>
> "CUE MUSIC," I heard though my earphones. Feeling faint, I did what I had to do.
>
> I just doubled the tempo and everything fit perfectly. As a matter of fact, it even sounded better than the original tempo. And like the wonderful studio musicians the performers were, they didn't even flinch.

CONSTRUCTING A COMPOSITION

*M*any times I've sat down at a desk or piano with pencils sharpened and music paper in front of me, just waiting for something to happen. And I wait. And wait. Then, maybe I hit a few keys, doodle a little bit and then something hits me. It's usually perspiration that brings it out, not inspiration.

What comes first? Melody? Harmony? A rhythmic pattern, perhaps? It really doesn't matter, just as long as something happens. And when that something happens, you've got a start. It may be feeble, but it's a start.

Now, if you're writing music on demand, such as a film score, a commission or something for a forthcoming record date, you can't monkey around too long. Get cracking, or you get fired. Those are the facts of commercial life.

I've often wondered about Ludwig van Beethoven. Did he wake up one morning and say, "I think I'll write the Fifth Symphony today." Did he hum

Dum - Dum - Dum   Dum

to himself, or did he just go to the piano and plunk it out? Another scenario: he was in a beer hall the night before, and a polka band played a catchy tune with those same four notes. Did he think, "Hmmm. . . maybe I could develop that?" Not only that, but I'll bet the more beers he had, the better it sounded!

It doesn't matter. What he did do was sit down with quill in hand and *write* the damn thing. That's the one thing you must eventually acknowledge as you sit there with your pencil and paper. You've got to write it.

Now we're at the point where there's no more passing the buck. MUSIC MUST BE WRITTEN. Furthermore, this book can't teach anyone how to compose music, nor can a teacher. In other words, unless you have the talent or the desire to develop the talent and skills, it will be very tough going. Obviously you wouldn't have bought this book if you weren't interested in composing, so let's go on to the next step.

Go to the piano and start wandering about. Better yet, *don't* go to the piano, but sit back in a comfortable chair instead and start thinking of a melody in your head. Sing it to yourself, then go to the piano and test it out. Even if it is similar to "Three Blind Mice" or "Twinkle, Twinkle, Little Star," you are on your way. Remember this if you get discouraged: there has probably never been a composer who didn't get frustrated the first time he or she decided to write a tune. So, there's nowhere to go but up.

Next you must decide what kind of piece you're going to write. What about the medium? Is it for a particular performance? Will there be limitations of difficulty? I think the hardest thing in the world is to compose a piece just for the sake of composing, but that's what a composer does. Painters have no guarantee that anyone will ever see their pictures displayed, nor do novelists have any guarantee that their books will be read. And composers have no guarantee that their music will be played, either. But if you're a real composer, you write music anyway.

Let's assume your local college orchestra asks you to write something for the annual spring concert. A five-minute work, programmatic or not. (Writing with a "program" in mind, such as a story, a scene of nature, industry, etc., makes a work programmatic. "Clair de Lune" is programmatic; Sonata no. 1 in E minor is not.) You jump at the chance because it will showcase your talent. You've got three months to write it, and with any luck you might eventually become rich and famous. Let's now assume that you'd like to do an "Americana" kind of work, a tone poem, if you will. It could be something with a western flavor, maybe a sort of *Rodeo*, à la Copland, or something that the Boston Pops might play.

This might be a good time to state that what we write is most assuredly a product of our experience. When I say "experience," I mean musical experience. I don't mean that we set out to plagiarize another writer's work but that, to a large extent, what we compose comes from our subconscious, and buried there is music that we've heard in the past.

Harmony comprises certain rules (with alterations, naturally) so that we all use the same chords and, to a great extent, in the same sequence. To make a point, no one can claim that a C chord followed by A minor, then D minor to G seventh is his or her own property. It is used constantly by everyone and is a part of our vocabulary. What we can try to make original, therefore, is the melody. One thing that makes a composition unique is a melody that is attractive, but different enough so that it doesn't sound like something that we already know.

Now that we've decided on a program piece, we have a little going for us. There are certain sounds and rhythms that come to mind when we think of the west—rodeos, broad vistas, and so on. We now have a broad tonal palette on which to create.

Before we attempt our melody we should consider the form or the structure of the piece. We could opt for an introduction (either short or extended), a main theme, a middle contrasting section and a return to the main theme. This is the basic ABA form, and it always works. We also could interpolate some interlude material and an extended ending that would borrow from all the thematic material. For the time being, let's go for an introduction and a straight ABA.

I usually write the introduction after I've finished the piece. By that time it practically writes itself because I've become so familiar with all the themes. We are at the point (whether we like it or not) where we need to come up with something. After fiddling around for a bit, I have come up with a theme.

After looking it over, I realize that the theme might be too short. An extension might help it to "breathe" a little better.

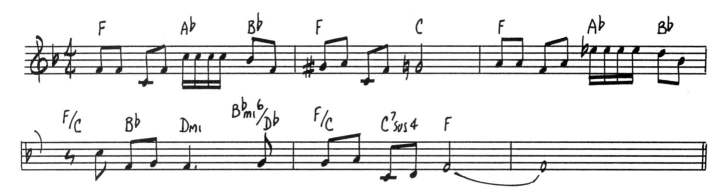

The chords are all quite simple. The only surprise is the use of the A-flat chord. The false cadence in measure 4 (D minor) is a nice touch and gives the piece a western feel. One might wonder why the last bar is a whole note (tied to its previous half-note), which runs contrary to the piece's rhythm. First of all, the phrase needs "air" before it is repeated, and it also allows space for a figure to be stated that will most likely be based on the theme. Besides, in this kind of music, a five-bar phrase would be awkward and, again, would not allow for the needed space.

Once you have a melody, you have implied harmony. Any note can be harmonized several ways, but usually there is only one that makes sense: the one that sounds right. The chords, at this point, will form a pattern that makes musical sense. This does not mean, however, that when you are developing the theme later in the piece, you cannot use chord substitutions. As a matter of fact, using these will show off your originality by introducing clever little surprises here and there.

Returning to our example, what makes this piece sound like Americana? For one thing, the use of the B-flat chord in place of a C chord is decidedly western. The skips in the melody are reminiscent of a square dance, and if it were executed very slowly with guitar strums, the material would sound quite folklike.

I remember a music publisher once telling me that a great melody requires only single notes on a piano to make it come to life. If you have to add harmony notes or the left hand, then something is missing in your melody.

That might be stretching the point, although this test would certainly work for Johann Strauss and Stephen Foster. Stravinsky and Prokofieff might run into a little trouble adhering to that philosophy, however.

The point is clear, nevertheless. The stronger your melody is, the less adornment you need. One could write a whole song using only C as the melody note, but harmonizing it with A-flat sevenths, F-major sevenths, B-flat ninths and so on. It might be moderately pleasing to the ear, but as a tune it certainly would be a dud.

So, when you've composed your theme, play it now and then without the chords. Does it have a line? Peaks and valleys? Can you make it more interesting by changing a note here and there? Addressing all these questions will help you to make your theme as strong and as memorable as possible.

When a lay person listens to music, it is usually the melody that's heard first and digested. Next is probably the rhythm, but in a subjective way only. Last is the harmony, as someone bereft of musical knowledge doesn't know what harmony is.

Some of my colleagues claim that orchestration is the first thing that an audience hears. That certainly may be the case, especially if it is a trumpet solo. But it would not be the case, however, if the whole orchestra were playing. What makes certain melodies last forever and others just fade away? It obviously is not just the orchestration, it is the melody.

The next step in our composition will be to add harmony. In this case, the harmonies flowed from the melody. As a matter of fact, I thought of the harmony *while* I was writing the melody; they seemed one and the same.

In this piece, the only place where different chords might work is the spot where the A-flat occurs. One could keep the F chord going as in this example:

It's okay. Simpler, of course, but not as exciting. (The previous F chord becomes an F⁷.)

Or, we could change the A-flat chord to an F chord with the third in the bass. Although it sounds fine and even more classical in approach, I think the A-flat is stronger. Here is that example:

We can certainly make things a little more complex if we wish. In measure 2 of the second example, the plain C chord could become a suspended fourth on the third beat, resolving on the fourth. We could also make it a seventh chord. In fact, both these things could be done on later expositions of the theme. Here it is:

The last six beats of the extended version give us an opportunity to create something different before we go back for a repeat. It could serve as a mini-interlude. Here are the last two bars embellished from their F-major tonality.

The next step in the process of creating our composition is the bass line. With music of this nature, the bass will be more-or-less obvious, but there are still choices. Let's go for the line that seems most logical:

Now let's try some substitutions. The new bass notes have a small arrow beneath them:

In changing the bass line, I also altered some chords. On the second beat of the first measure, we now have a G-minor seventh. It should probably be spelled as a C seventh, with a suspended fourth with G in the bass. The reason for this is that the D in the G-minor seventh is excess baggage.

I did not change the sequence in measure 4 where we have the descending pattern of D minor, B-flat minor with the D-flat in the bass, and the F chord with its bass note of C. Stepwise bass patterns always sound good, and the F with the C in the bass helps to set up our final cadence.

The previous example might be a little too busy for the first exploitation of the theme. We can save it for later if we wish, perhaps toward the end.

Always remember that the bass is just that; it becomes the basis of the melody and harmony. Voice-leading in the bass is important; awkward and constant skips do not make for smooth sailing. If you are not satisfied with the bass in its root position, play around with the inversions. An example of that follows, where the C-seventh chord is used with the fifth in the bass. The root-position version follows:

The first example just seems to flow better. However, if the first F chord were in root position rather than in the first inversion (third in the bass), then the second example would work better. The piano and organ works of Bach are a great place to study root movements and voice-leading. Time spent studying them will never be wasted.

Before we go on, let's address the eventual harmonization of our melody notes. Everything is straightforward except for the nonchordal notes that appear. Those notes are as follows:

In measure 2, the F chord with the G-sharp in the melody can be handled in one of three ways: as a diminished D chord (my least favorite), or as an F chord with the G-sharp replacing the A. Finally, it could be written as an E-major chord retaining the F bass. Here is what they look like:

The next two examples in measures 4 and 5 are easier to deal with. They become F-major ninth chords without the major seventh, the E. Why eliminate that note? Because it would sound too "jazzy" or rich for the style of the piece. Another possibility would be to replace the A in the melody with the G. Here are the two examples:

One of the top studio trumpet players in Hollywood, whom we shall call "Bill" for the purpose of this story, was appearing with Lawrence Welk when Welk was on ABC television.

During one of the telecasts, Bill had a solo and took a few liberties with the melody by interpolating a few jazz ad-libs that were consistent with the music.

After the show, Welk called him into his dressing room. "That was a nice solo you played, my boy, but I noticed you played some jazz licks and didn't stick to the melody. You should forget that kind of music. Look what happened to Benny Goodman, he played jazz all his life and never got anywhere."

Assuming that we will repeat our main theme, it will still be too short before it segues into our slow theme, the "B" part of our A-B-A form. Not only that, but it will sound incomplete. So we are going to modify our structure with a secondary theme that will return to our main theme before moving into our slow section. This secondary theme will be in the same tempo and style. Our form of the composition has now been altered to create an ABA form for the first section.

What I have done is to write a new theme in the key of B-flat that I hope will complement our first theme. In actuality, this theme is more of an interlude or "breakup" strain that will take us back to our original in the key of F. As you will note, no modulation is required.

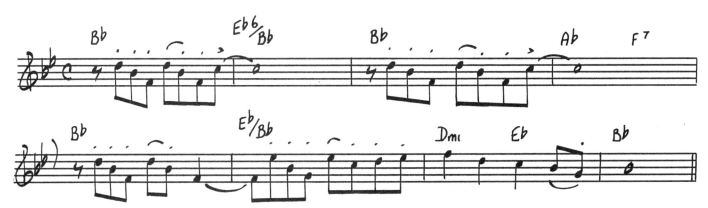

Note that I kept the B-flat bass as a pedal for the first three measures. Again, this is a device used quite often in music of a western nature. Using this pedal was strictly subjective on my part; the root would also be fine. Our interlude theme could be repeated (with a slightly different orchestration) before going back to the first statement, but it is not necessary. Its only purpose is to provide contrast and make the total composition more complete.

Here, now, is our secondary theme with bass notes:

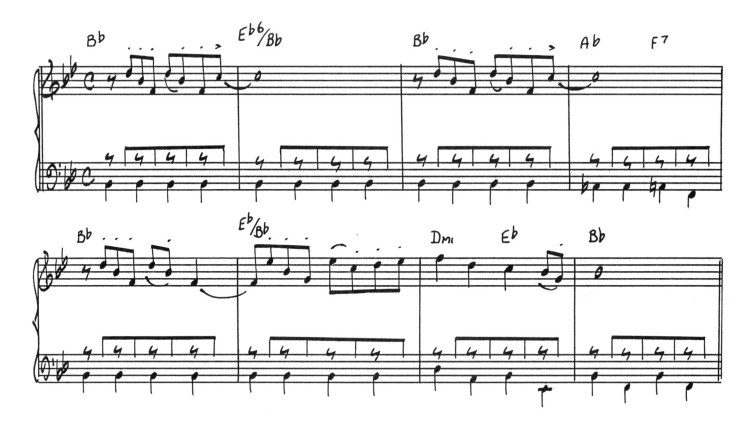

Notice that in measure 4, the F seventh uses the third in the bass before jumping to the root.

So, to sum up what we have done so far: we have a main theme that is repeated and moves to our secondary theme, which will then return to the original. What we have is a strict ABA form for our first section.

It is now time to go to our broad, slow middle section. It is obvious that we cannot do it abruptly, so let us compose a small bridge that will take us into the introduction of our middle theme. One way to do this is to have the small coda effect a ritard, which gradually paves the way to the new tempo; the other way is to do it abruptly. I have chosen the abrupt way, as I want to keep the fast rhythm going and let the melody and orchestration telegraph the forthcoming change. Here is our bridge, which also serves, by the way, as a modulation. Although a modulation is not mandatory, I think it helps to create our new mood. The modulation is from the key of F to the key of C.

The modulation becomes effective on the third beat of measure 2 with the sounding of the G chord with the F in the bass. By repeating the harmonic content in measure 3, we firmly establish the new key of C. The last beat of measure 4, the G-seventh chord, will resolve on the downbeat of the start of our new theme.

Note the C-major chord at the beginning of the two-measure introduction to the slow theme. It contains a major ninth and sixth, which convey a strong feeling of the outdoors and spaciousness. The melody and harmony are very simple, and I have attempted to create a western flavor tinged with feelings of folksy Americana.

As for nonchordal tones in this section, there is little that is complicated. In music of this nature there is basically only one way to handle these notes without getting tricky. What we are looking for is simplicity. The arrows designate the nonchordal tones.

The other way to handle the harmonization of nonchordal tones is to use chord substitutions. In this case, however, I would like to be faithful to the original harmonies and keep the nonchordal tones "passing" through our harmony. Our pattern seems to be one chord per bar; this way of handling the passing tones seems consistent with the structure. Now that we have the melodies and harmonies of our themes, we must apply ourselves to the creation of moving lines that will compliment the music. Commonly referred to as countermelodies, these lines make the difference between just a song and a composition. Although the counter does not have to be memorable in its own right, it should flow and ebb with the melody. It is not necessary to make the counterline "too busy;" now and then it can rest and sustain.

The counter should not be in the same register as the melody, or it will lose its distinctiveness. There should be at least a one-octave difference, perhaps even two. Such is the case, for example, when you have high violins with the cellos playing a counter two octaves below. When it comes time to orchestrate your music, you must select sections that will come out on their own without interfering with the main theme. Very few solo instruments, with the exception of the French horn, are capable of stating a counter on their own. (This does not apply to thin or solo sections.)

Just because you introduced a counter with one section doesn't mean you have to stick with it. You could start off with low strings and switch to horns later on. When the melody goes to low instruments, then high woodwinds could take over the function. Be adventurous! If something is held for too long, it gets boring.

Although I tend to like unison counters, if you have a full-blown tutti going, woodwinds in octaves can be very effective. The same thing goes for strings. Nothing is more exciting than a huge symphonic ensemble playing concerted material, with the strings in three octaves soaring above it in dramatic counterpoint. In the pages to follow, I will attempt to demonstrate examples of this craft. I'm sure that with a little practice you will be able to improve upon them.

> *The late Max Winkler was not only the founder and president of Belwin, Inc., but also a great storyteller and raconteur. He was holding court one day at the Chicago Midwest Band Clinic at the Sherman Hotel, and was surrounded by a group of band directors and educators. I was also in the group, listening to his stories. At one point he said that he built the success of his band-music publishing empire by publishing only those works that were rejected by other publishers.*
>
> *I couldn't let that pass.*
>
> *"Then, sir," I said, looking him directly in the eye, "you will never publish anything of mine."*

CREATING A COUNTERMELODY

If a countermelody (or counterpoint) were to move in exactly the same rhythm as the melody it would serve as harmony. Several countermelodies moving independently, such as in a fugue, create harmony as they pass in and out, but they are still counterpoint.

The simplest rule of thumb in creating countermelodies is this: when the melody is sustained, you move your line. When the melody moves, you sustain your line. The countermelody will always be heard second behind the melody, because the melody is usually stated first. The countermelody should enhance the main theme, never confusing it or competing with it. This is even more important when a second countermelody is introduced. When we get beyond one such secondary theme, then we are entering the area of modified canons and fugues.

We must also be aware of what the ear can assimilate in one hearing. As a composer or arranger, you will go over the material in your mind or at the piano countless times. For the audience, it's only once. Keep that in mind. Keep it simple. Countermelodies are great places to use passing tones and suspensions. I love suspensions. I like to think that subliminally they keep listeners (and performers as well) on the edge of their seats. Exaggerated perhaps, but a suspension delays the inevitable, a final resolution.

> *Robert Russell Bennett was indeed the dean of the Broadway orchestrators. (Orchestrator is perhaps a misnomer, as that term represents someone who merely transfers a complete musical sketch to a full score.) No, Bennett was a gifted arranger. (This term designates someone who does the whole thing from scratch— no sketch, just a lead sheet with chord symbols.) Although he worked primarily for Rodgers and Hammerstein, he did work for other theater composers now and then. There is one delightful tidbit that certainly bears repeating. In 1944, Billy Rose had produced a show called "The Seven Lively Arts," which encom-*

passed all the performing arts. For the ballet, Rose had commissioned Igor Stravinsky to do a fifteen-minute ballet, which the celebrated composer promptly delivered.

After the opening in Philadelphia, Rose, whose ego knew no bounds, sent Stravinsky a telegram as follows: "YOUR MUSIC GREAT SUCCESS—STOP—COULD BE SENSATIONAL SUCCESS IF YOU WOULD AUTHORIZE ROBERT RUSSELL BENNETT RETOUCH ORCHESTRATION—STOP—BENNETT ORCHESTRATES EVEN THE WORKS OF COLE PORTER—STOP."

Stravinsky wired back: "SATISFIED WITH GREAT SUCCESS."

Because we haven't included a chapter on harmony as such, this might be a good time to sound off on a favorite subject of mine: suspensions. Once you hit a dominant chord, especially a dominant seventh, the game is over. You're home. You can fake it sometimes. For example, if you are in the key of F and sound your C seventh, you would normally go to the F chord for the ending. If you resolve it to a D minor, you have created a false cadence. But, after horsing around a little bit more, you will still eventually reach the ending. One way to delay the resolution is to substitute the F for the E in your dominant seventh; you can go anywhere.

The effect of the suspension is to conceal the tonality of the chord. There are many types, and they all do the same thing (with the exception, perhaps, of the suspended 13th in a dominant chord that eventually resolves to the fifth).

The resolution of any suspension provides relief. So if you want suspense (from where the word originates), use them sparingly. They impart a slight dissonance and "edge" to your harmony and are especially effective in pop music.

The most common type of suspension is the suspended fourth in a dominant chord, which resolves to the third, like this:

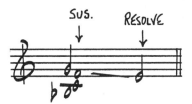

Another type is the suspended ninth in a major chord, which, again, usually resolves upward to the third.

Another type of suspension is the 13th in a dominant chord, which moves down to the fifth.

Bear in mind that the suspension creates a "holding" pattern that delays the inevitable resolution. This, however, is not etched in stone; it is possible to get to the tonic without ever going to the third of the dominant. It's just a different sound.

As we create a countermelody for our main theme, it looks as if we will be mainly sustaining (rather than moving) because of the active nature of the melody. What I have come up with certainly works harmonically and rhythmically, but it is no great shakes as a melody unto itself. Regardless, our intent is to create an accompaniment. The most melodic we can get here is in the last two measures, where the melody truly sustains. Regarding the orchestration of this passage, the countermelody would be excellent for violas and cellos (assuming we are using woodwinds in the melody). Just by luck, the counter is in the right range for both these string instruments. Had it gone one note lower, it would have been out of range for the violas. Another way to treat it would be perhaps with a clarinet solo on the melody and a bassoon on the counter, which would be a more subtle and personal treatment of the music. (A solo instrument runs the risk of competing with the melody.)

Now that we've created a countermelody, it is time to consider another countermelody that can be interpolated during a repeat of the theme, or maybe even at the end of the composition. What we see next is simpler and more sustained than our original one, but it nevertheless adds a new dimension to our piece. It also helps to fill out the harmony. If you go through the section you will see that most of the harmony in each chord is supplied by our countermelodies. In other words, we have created a horizontal, or linear, harmonic texture without reverting to the more simple solution of just placing sustained harmony under our melody, which any fool can do.

What we have done is *composing*, not arranging. The original theme could be called a song or a tune, but when we create the lines to accompany it, we have become composers.

As a little addendum to the following sketch, one would probably incorporate some afterbeats, which could further fill out our harmonies.

Because we have constructed countermelodies and moved patterns around, our middle theme is easier because of its slow tempo. The melody (which could be a French or English horn solo) is in the treble clef with the stems down. In measure 11, the melody could be taken over by the high violins. At measure 15, I added the entire string section in three octaves.

Although the basic countermelody is in the bass clef (stems up), you will note that I added another countermelody (in the treble clef above the melody), which could be played during the repeat. To introduce them at the same time might be a little confusing to the ear.

At measure 11, the counter could be played by woodwinds for three bars. I added sustaining notes (which could be played by trombones) and introduced an eighth-note arpeggiated pattern in the harp (or perhaps guitar). At measure 14, the horns (accented) enter and play along with the strings for a stronger presentation of the melody.

So what do we do at measure 15? All the strings are on the melody, and the horns are tied over from measure 14. My solution is to have the horns take over the melody (along with the violas) on the third beat of the measure, and to let the cellos and bassoons play the countermelody.

My choices for the orchestration are all subjective, but they work. For example, instead of a horn (or English horn) solo at the beginning, it could just as well be a woodwind tutti. The counter at this point would work well for violas and cellos.

COUNTERMELODY ADDED TO MIDDLE THEME

At measure 11 (where we go into a kind of "beat"), a way to create movement would be to create a pattern, such as the following, either for violas or horns. Violas, however, would be more subtle and characteristic of the music. Short afterbeats would be inappropriate (because of the slow tempo), but a guitar playing the rhythm would be just dandy.

The following examples show other treatments of countermelodies. In "Days of Glory," the melody is in the cornets with the woodwinds stating the counter theme. The low pedal point (B-flat) helps to underpin the whole thing.

Days of Glory

Words by
Edward Heyman

Music by
John Cacavas

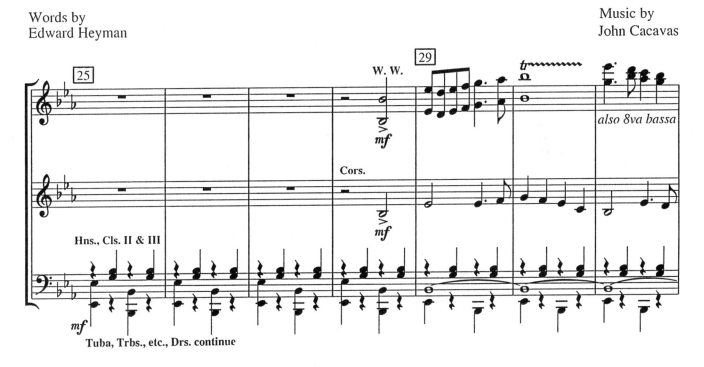

F528-66

The next example, "American Concertette," contains a more legato and
flowing subject. The counter is in the third clarinets, alto clarinet and horns. In
the fifth bar, the horns only play the counter.

American Concertette

FULL SCORE
Duration – 5:30

John Cacavas

In the next example, a march treatment of "Give My Regards to Broadway," the melody is concerted with the brass, and the high woodwinds are playing the countermelody. This is a good example of the "move-sustain" method. The counter is pitched high, and the piccolo, sounding an octave higher, gives it a two-octave spread.

Star Spangled Spectacular
The Music of George M. Cohan

CONDENSED SCORE
Duration – 4:30

George M. Cohan
Arranged by John Cacavas

Perhaps now is the time to go back over what we have done and put it into perspective. Here is what we have so far:

1. Main theme (A)

2. Repeat of main theme

3. Interlude theme (B) (with optional repeat)

4. Main theme (A) returns

5. Bridge

6. Middle slow theme (C), preceded by a two-measure introduction

What remains now is to write some kind of transition that will take us back to our original statement. It is certainly possible to do without the transition, but its inclusion will make it a better piece. Next, we must write an ending or coda that will tell everybody that we are heading for the finish line. Still to be written is the introduction, which will probably contain some of our thematic material.

We must also consider whether we want to return to the original key of F or get really tricky and move to another key. One solution to our transition would be to extend the ending of the slow section or to effect a modulation and return to our earlier bridge. An additional touch would be to add a few measures that contain only a rhythmic pattern before we state our original theme. I think that's the way to go. Let's pick it up at the *fine* which is nine measures from the end of the previous example.

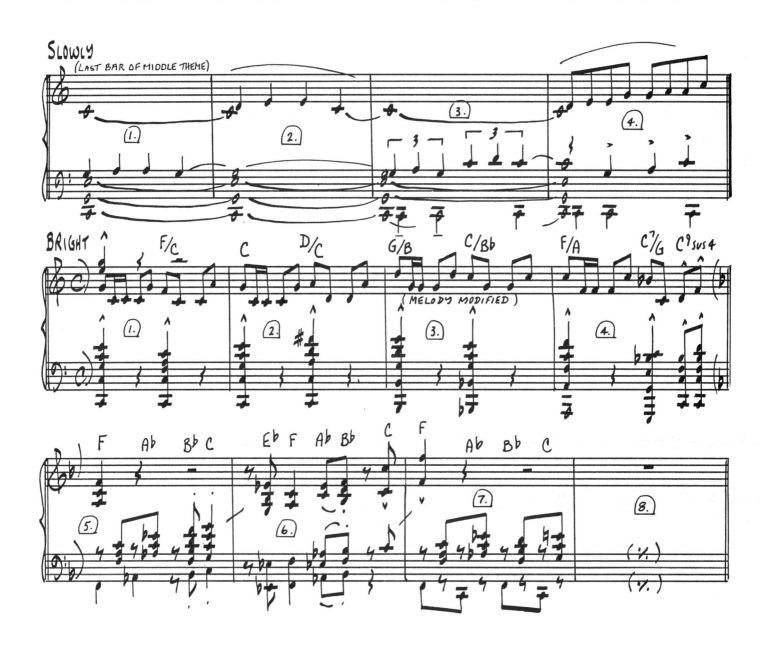

As you can see, we are using a four-measure transition before we get to our bridge sequence. Note that the momentum of the quarter-note pattern increases to triplets in measure 3 and eighth-notes in measure 4. This has the effect of preparing us for the fast tempo that begins at measure 1. There is no real melody in measures 1 through 4, just the motion of notes. I kept these four measures in the tonality of C, which is just one way of handling it. For example, measures 2 and 4 could just as well have been B-flat chords with an added C.

When we get to the transition at measure 1, obviously it will be fully scored. The first two measures are the same harmonically and melodically as when they were first used. But now we must get back to the key of F. The melody and harmony are modified in measures 3 and 4 to accommodate this key change. The actual modulation occurs on the third beat of measure 3 with the C chord and its B-flat bass. The last two beats of measure 4 firm up the modulation.

Measures 5–8 are the last section of this bridge. This section helps to set up the rhythm of our main theme reprise that is to follow. It is similar to a square dance in character, with a harmonic approach that's a little more sophisticated.

We are now on the home stretch. Our main theme gets reprised with a repeat. We then have to fashion an ending and start working on the introduction. Leaving the introduction until the end is always a good idea. That way you can pick and choose from your best thematic material. At this time we will work on the ending.

To analyze our ending, we see that the first three measures are all basically variations on our main theme. Measure 4 comes from some of our bridge material, and the last three measures comprise new material that is, again, based on past harmonies.

The downbeat of measure 1 (heavily accented) marks the last beat of the main theme.

The trumpets and horns carry the melody until the entrance of the strings and woodwinds in the last half of measure 2. Note the use of the added second in measure 1. This keeps the harmony rather neutral until the suspended chord in measure 2. Also, for what it is worth, we did not end with any kind of dominant seventh leading to the tonic. We could have done so, however, by making the E-flat chord (with the low C pedal) change to a C-major chord on the fourth beat of measure 5.

So there we have our ending. It is just one solution among many that could have been employed, but I think the summation of the piece is well served by what we have. Nothing really new has been added, which helps to tie everything together.

Notice that the beginning is scored a little sparsely, with more instruments and colors gradually added until the full tutti at measure 4. The trill in the woodwinds was added as an afterthought to create excitement; it is strictly optional.

In the late sixties I wrote a concert march called "Gallant Men." It was moderately successful, and little did I realize what would happen when Charles Osgood, the well-known CBS news commentator, decided to write a lyric to it.

"Then what?" I asked.

"We'll get Senator Everett Dirksen to record it," he answered nonchalantly.

I thought the tropical sun or the rum was getting to him, as we were both vacationing in the Virgin Islands with our respective families.

"If he turns it down, maybe we could get the Beatles to do it," I said somewhat sarcastically.

Well, the senator did record it, along with his recitations to "The Star Spangled Banner," "The Gettysburg Address," and several other patriotic readings.

It sold a million dollars' worth in about three weeks.

With the large and unexpected success of the album Gallant Men, *Capitol Records thought a Christmas album with the senator might do very well. We selected a group of carols, and I busied myself orchestrating them for an orchestra and mixed choir.*

We had all congregated at the A & R studios in Manhattan on a summer day in 1967, and it was bedlam. The ABC television network was there with a large crew; Look Magazine *had decided to do a feature story on the recording session, and there were the frustrated engineers trying to set up microphones and platforms.*

All of a sudden, the senator came bursting through the doors amid the flashing of cameras and assorted oohs and ahhs from various people in the studio.

I was on the podium adjusting my earphones as he came in. He gave me a wink and headed right for the female singers who were on the opposite side of the studio doing a voice check. He grabbed several of the girls, put his arms around them and bestowed a few kisses. There were several cheers and whistles at this display of affection. Once a politician, always a politician, I thought. Those guys can get away with anything. As he started walking back to the podium, I heard a few giggles from the women through my headset. And then one of them said, "That old coot French-kissed me!"

The senator headed for my podium and perched himself on a stool to my right. He leaned over and said, "You know, this is a helluva lot more fun than politics!"

THE INTRODUCTION

For a work of this length, an eight-measure introduction is certainly adequate, although a couple of measures could be added with no problem. Twelve measures, however, might be too much.

What I have done is returned to our main theme and slow theme for the basic material of the introduction. In measures 1, 2 and 3, I broadened the rhythmic values and waited until the fourth measure to add the 16th notes. Measure 5 brings in our middle theme, quite rich and broad, with the same countermelodies we used in the construction of the theme.

A fermata could be added on the last note of the introduction, but I think a ritard would serve the same purpose.

The opening is quite exciting, with a woodwind eighth-note pattern along with the strings' tremolo. Note that no matter what chord we are using in the first four measures, this ostinato pattern will work against it. If we had the third in this pattern, it would not work at all. It is not until the fifth measure that we hear the pure harmony of a major triad, and with the large three-octave string unison entering, it will be a nice sound indeed. Needless to say, the addition of percussion, especially suspended cymbal and timpani, will add to the grandiose effect.

Although I say "violins" in the first four measures, the violas should certainly be added on the lower note.

When the performers get to the first beat of the main theme, after the introduction, make sure they come in with a bang!

Our piece is now complete. Review it in its rough form, and look for ways to make it better. Chances are, you'll find some. Make sure legato lines flow into one another and that the voice leading is as good as you can get it.

The next step will be to make your condensed score, which will also serve as a conductor part. You will add the dynamics and percussion and, as you go along, check for wrong notes. Don't forget measure numbers and/or rehearsal letters.

Once your sketch is completed, you might want to leave everything alone for a day or so. When you go back to it, you'll have a fresher view and will be better equipped to deal with any changes you might want to make.

Now to the full score. Make sure your paper will accommodate whatever you want, especially percussion lines. If you've included a harp, make sure you have two staves for that instrument. Even if you didn't include a harp, write the part anyway. The next performance might use one.

If you are short of staves, certain instruments can be combined on one staff, such as trumpets, trombones and clarinets. Two horns are usually put on a single staff anyway. When you divide the strings, remember: stems up and stems down. And never divide the basses; it's a dumb move.

We haven't discussed the piano, but it would certainly be a nice touch. Make sure it's optional—and again, you might have a problem getting score paper to accommodate it along with a harp.

Regarding the orchestration, you will have a good idea of what to do by this time. In many of the examples, I have offered suggestions for what instruments to use, and this is where your skill comes into focus. Our piece, although light in nature, is constructed along classical lines. The instruments, too, are playing in the classical mode. You will have many options in orchestrating this. Just go for the ones that make the most sense, and don't overdo any one section.

GOOD LUCK!

Arnold Schoenberg, the father of the twelve-tone system of music composition, emigrated to America during World War II. Like Stravinsky, he settled in Los Angeles. As he was a famous composer at this time, it was only inevitable that he would get a call from a movie studio. He was approached by Irving Thalberg, the production chief of MGM, and agreed to attend a screening of a motion picture. It was Thalberg's hope that Schoenberg would agree to score it. After seeing the picture, Schoenberg went home and said he would be in touch. Soon Thalberg received a letter from Schoenberg saying that he would be happy to write music for the movies, but he had a better plan. Schoenberg suggested that he write two hours of music, to which MGM would shoot a film based around his score.

He never heard back from MGM, or from any other studio.

THE WOODWIND SECTION

*T*wo flutes, two oboes, two clarinets and two bassoons are the usual complement of a symphony orchestra's woodwind section. There are many doubles, such as piccolo, English horn, bass clarinet and contrabassoon, and many orchestras have extra utility players. Some modern scores call for more than the normal grouping.

In the symphonic band, many clarinets are used, with the addition of bass and alto clarinets, plus at least four saxophones and, now and then, the contrabass clarinet.

The woodwinds, as a section, have a great range, possess few problems of articulation and are capable of producing many different colors. With the exception of the piccolo, however, they lack power. That little instrument, by the way, can be heard distinctly above a huge orchestra or band playing double fortissimo. As an isolated group, the woodwinds do not blend together particularly well, although groupings within them can be very effective (flutes and clarinets, for example, and low clarinets and bassoons).

The flute's lowest notes are practically inaudible, and for that reason alto and bass flutes are used quite often in recording. The extreme low notes of oboes are hard to play and are often grating on the ear. The high notes of a bassoon, especially when played by a fine player, are quite attractive.

The colors of these instruments make them solo favorites much more than, for example, trumpets or trombones, and the symphonic repertoire is filled with such solo examples. Unless one is writing for a recording, great care must be taken when writing solos for winds. Although a high clarinet can cut through an ensemble, there is only so much volume that can be achieved in a flute solo. The same can be said for the English horn and bassoon. The oboe, with its piercing tone quality, is more audible. Let's just say that you would treat a background for a woodwind solo quite differently from that for a brass solo.

The saxophones, which are so important to jazz bands and pop music, have never really been part of the conventional symphony orchestra. Many composers, such as Maurice Ravel, have incorporated them into their scores, but there is hardly anything written for them in this area as a section.

Saxophones are a mainstay of concert and marching bands and have recently gained more visibility in rock music. They are extremely expressive and are capable of producing many colors. Like flutes and strings, they sound entirely different when played without vibrato. If vibrato is used in a concert band's sax section to play something serious rather than pop music, the instrument will sound strange. In other words, vibrato must be turned on and off depending on what they are playing.

Writing for the winds as a section requires a little thought. If the flute is playing the melody, it can get lost quite easily. One of my favorite voicings is having one oboe on the melody. To make this work, the melody must be in a fairly high range. The flutes are placed below the oboe, and the clarinets below the flutes. The second oboe is tacet.

When two oboes and two bassoons play together as a concerted section, you end up hearing two oboes and two bassoons. Interesting, but not a blend.

Quite often woodwinds are used to bolster the strings. This technique has been around from the very beginning and works best in loud, fully orchestrated passages. Because of the inherent dichotomy between the sounds of the two sections, be careful when using the two sections together in transparent, soft passages. In contemporary writing this technique is less prevalent than in the classical repertoire.

The following example shows a concerted woodwind section playing an ostinato figure. Note that the flute and piccolo (sounding an octave higher) have the melody, while the clarinets are in three-part harmony. The E-flat clarinet, which is not used much anymore, is also playing the melody. In this particular example, the bells are playing with the piccolo.

Symphonic Scenario

By John Cacavas
A. S. C. A. P.

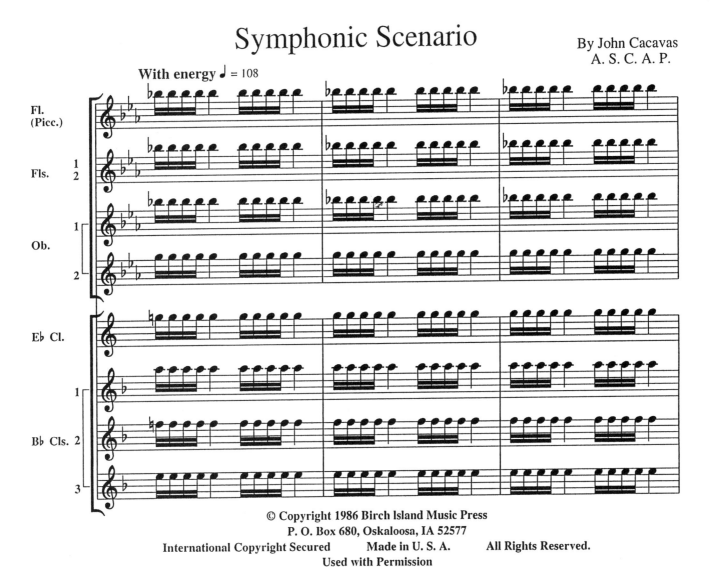

The next example is quite similar, although the oboes are not playing the melody but doubling the clarinets. It is a fortissimo passage with the snare drum playing the same figure and the trumpets doubling the clarinets an octave lower. Note that the clarinets are all voiced in their upper registers. Anything below their "break" (B-flat) would be completely inaudible.

American Concertette

FULL SCORE
Duration – 5 : 30

John Cacavas

Thirds in the woodwinds are always effective and pleasant to the ear. The following example contains the flutes and piccolo in the top octave, the oboes and clarinets in the middle octave and the saxes in the bottom octave. This excerpt is for a concert band arrangement. If it were for orchestra, the bassoons would probably play the sax parts. This example would certainly sound all right with just the thirds played by the top woodwinds, but the addition of the bottom octave gives it more support and substance.

Legions
(Concert March)

Duration – 4 : 00

John Cacavas

Q. M. B. 507

Printed in U. S. A.

Another sound that is very sonorous is that of the low woodwinds in two parts, one on the melody, the others on a countermelody. The following example encompasses both of these, plus a third sustaining line. The total harmony is created by these three parts. This voicing would work for any family, such as horns and trombones, and of course, a low string section. This, again, happens to be scored for concert band. Note the broad phrasing in the woodwinds; I tried to make it as orchestral in scope as possible. At one point as I was writing this piece I was tempted to give the alto clarinet or bassoon a four-bar phrase also, but because this piece was for a school band, I decided against it. All the clarinets keep the melody going, so the effect still works. The example starts at measure 15.

Arthur Schwartz composed some of America's best-loved and most successful songs. Among others, his lyricists were Howard Dietz, Dorothy Fields, Ira Gershwin and Johnny Mercer. "Dancing in the Dark," "That's Entertainment," "You and the Night and the Music" and "Haunted Heart" were just a few of them. His biggest hit was probably "Dancing in the Dark," which has had millions of performances and has been recorded several hundred times by various artists.

During the seventies Schwartz moved to London. He had been a longtime Anglophile and felt that he might find a fresh approach to his work. After he had been there for a short time, he decided to make demonstration records of some of his songs in a more contemporary, updated manner. Although his songs had made him very wealthy, he was not getting any of the younger performers to record them. True, he had a lot of album inclusions by artists like Frank Sinatra and Tony Bennett, but he was hungry for a hit single.

On this particular evening, he was in the studio putting the finishing touches on "Dancing in the Dark." A rock-and-roll band had performed the song, and the engineer, who was probably about twenty years old, had done a very fine job. Schwartz was pleased with the outcome. Everyone was relaxing, listening to the playback, and when they were about to leave the studio, the young engineer asked Schwartz, "That's a very nice song, sir. Is it yours?"

Schwartz, somewhat taken aback, replied, "Why yes."

"I just want to wish you a lot of luck with it," said the engineer.

The Fourth of July

John Cacavas

Another example of woodwind choir writing is this setting of "Annie Laurie." It starts off with just the clarinets, alto and bass clarinets and bassoons. Four measures later the flutes are sustained above them. (Note that I did not use the oboes; I wanted a very soft and haunting color and felt the oboes would intrude.) Another way of approaching this situation, however, would be to introduce an oboe solo at the end of measure 48 that's an octave higher than the first clarinet.

In Chapter 10 I give an example of simplifying a rapid woodwind passage by alternating the 16th-note pattern. Here is another example of this device:

Parada Mexicana

FULL SCORE
Duration – 4 : 30

John Cacavas

Here is another problem: we have a 16th-note pattern that is repeated for quite a while, something like this:

Rather than wear everybody out, we write the pattern in eighth and 16ths (and vice versa). The third clarinet plays a simpler part but does not interfere with the final result. Here is a concert sketch:

Another very effective form of overlapping can be found in the march from Tchaikovsky's *Nutcracker Suite*. In this case, it is the strings that are divided on their entrances, overlapping as they make their ascent.

To make a four-part concerted arrangement straight up and down doesn't require a lot of thought. It also won't be very interesting. In the following example, from *Traumeri*, I tried to extend the scope of four clarinets yet keep everything simple, as the collection of arrangements seemed to require. In other words, I tried to give the four clarinets the scope of an orchestra.

Traumeri

By R. SCHUMANN
Arranged by John Cacavas

When writing trills for woodwinds (or any other instruments, for that matter), be sure to indicate which note is the principal note. The following example, from a section of Mussorgsky's *Boris Godunov*, spells it out very clearly. What is interesting is that only the melody is trilling; the harmony parts are playing it straight. The example starts in the second measure. If you notice the last two beats of the example, the second and third clarinets trill on the B-flat, although they haven't been trilling before.

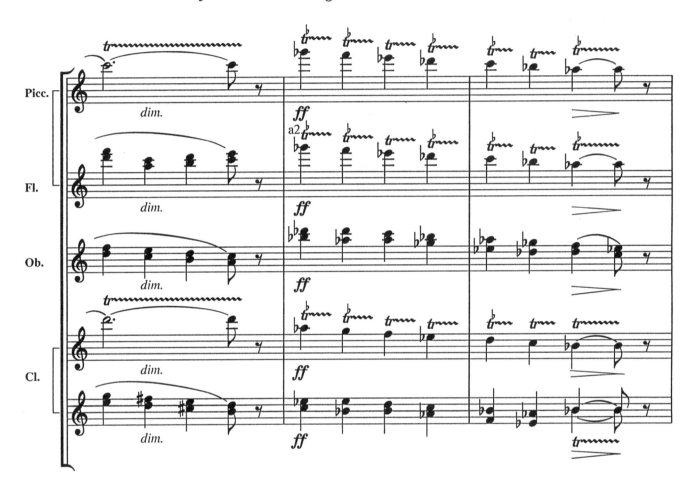

Sometimes a composer lets the key signature of the piece dictate how the trills are executed and resolved. I think it is better to mark them. That way you won't waste time during rehearsals for needless questions.

Many years ago I was appearing at the Tri-State Music Festival in Enid, Oklahoma, sharing the bill with a well-known conductor. This gentleman was a very elegant dresser and famous for his sartorial splendor. We were all quite friendly during rehearsals and the concert promised to be quite exciting. We had a massed band of hundreds and an orchestra and chorus numbering several more hundred, and thousands were expected at the concert.

For my dress that evening, I had brought along a black velvet suit that had been made for me by the Beatles' tailor in London. I guess in the back of my mind I wanted to give my colleague a little competition. Well, when I walked out to take my bow, and the spotlights hit that velvet suit, I received a five-minute ovation just for the suit, even before I gave a downbeat. After the applause subsided a little, I opened my jacket, which revealed a bright-red silk lining. As you can imagine, pandemonium broke loose and another few minutes of applause erupted. I looked offstage left to see my fellow conductor seething at this display. After all, he was wearing a mere thousand-dollar tuxedo.

On the flight back to New York he pointedly avoided me and spoke not a word.

THE BRASS SECTION

I remember at the age of thirteen asking my father to buy me a saxophone. He suggested I consider the trumpet instead. When I asked him why, he said that it would be much easier to play because it had only three keys (valves).

Well, as we all know, when you press a sax key down the note is there. With a trumpet it's a little dicey. The note just might *not* be there.

The trumpets are bright, and by their very nature, exposed. You can hide a little if you're in the back of the fiddle section, but with a shiny brass trumpet you stand out. Stark naked. Make a mistake and everybody looks at you. Even the audience, who will let an out-of-tune note pass on a clarinet or ignore a clinker hit on the piano, will snicker when the trumpet goes bloop. Not only that, playing the trumpet takes stamina. Gotta take your vitamins or you'll never make it. And you just might get fat cheeks. Look at Dizzy Gillespie. It has occurred to me that if he had it to do all over again, he might have opted for an accordion. In other words, it's a horn for the brave. A lot of things can go wrong. I remember a surgeon in New York telling me that if it weren't for trumpet players he'd be out of business in the hernia department. He also said that with the craze for electric guitars, he had noticed a slight decline in patients and, like the rest of us, had fond hopes for the return of the big bands. . . though his reasons were more material.

So down to brass tacks, as they say. When you voice three trumpets in three-part harmony, leave out the least important note. If it is a C-seventh chord, leave out the G, unless it's the melody. In that case, leave out the root. If it's a C-sixth chord, leave out the sixth and put it someplace else. If it's a ninth chord, again leave out the G. Here is a group of voicings that sound effective.

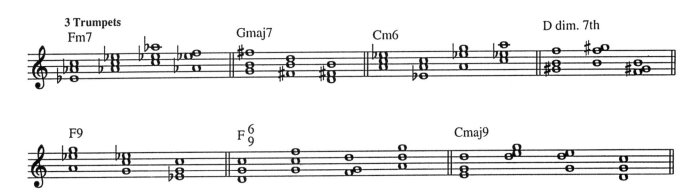

From the preceding examples you can see that if there is a four-note chord, then one note must be left out. If we have four trumpets, our problem has disappeared. In the diminished-chord example, I left out the root, although theoretically a diminished seventh chord has no root. Let's say that we leave out the bass note, which one can assume would be somewhere in the orchestration.

My choice of voicings is subjective, although they work quite well. Sometimes the choice of notes will depend on what else is happening in the score.

In the G-major seventh example, you'll see that there is no chord with the G in the melody. To put an F-sharp below it is just a little too strong, in my opinion. However, it could work in a sax section or with strings.

In the case of chords with an added sixth, unless you have four voices, you'll just end up with a minor chord. It would be best to give the three trumpets a straight triad and insert the sixth somewhere else. Keep in mind when writing harmony for trumpets that the chord should be complete within the section. Do not rely on another instrument to fill in an important note; it will be a poor substitute.

If you carry these voicings over to the piano and play through them, it will all make sense. Each situation has a different rule, and that's what makes it interesting. Sometimes you leave out the fifth, sometimes you don't.

TRUMPETS

When writing unisons for trumpets, give yourself some leeway. If it's a very high passage and you don't have top professionals playing it, give the third trumpet an optional part (e.g., the original high part plus the line an octave lower)—assuming, of course, that the line will also be an octave lower. If not, just cue the third trumpet. If that trumpeter's got nerve and the ability, he or she will play it.

Of all the brass instruments, the trumpets have the ability to articulate the most easily, much more so than the trombones or horns. When writing concerted passages for the brass section, please keep this in mind. Just because trumpets can triple-tongue doesn't mean that other members of the brass section can do it too.

Trumpets in the extreme low register are not particularly attractive. In unison, with the bells covered, a satisfactory effect can be achieved, but don't overdo it. The same rule applies to everyone. Extreme ranges are not where it's at. There are exceptions, of course, like the lowest notes of the trombone and strings, for example, but most other instruments do not take kindly to this kind of mistreatment.

If you're using top professionals and need or want low trumpets, switch them to flugelhorn, which gives you a sound between the horns and trombones. Even then, your options are limited. They can't go too high, and the low notes tend to be muddy, just like their higher cousins, the trumpets. Write for these instruments in their proper ranges and you'll never go wrong. Just remember that there are not that many Maynard Fergusons out there.

One last thought: don't have the trumpets play all the time. Give them plenty of time to rest the old lip, and to change mutes—and remember what I said about the hernias.

*One day in London, Louis Dreyfus —who, along with his brother
Max, controlled the vast music-publishing empire of Chappell—
came storming out of his office in a state of great agitation.*

"CATASTROPHE!" he shouted. "CATASTROPHE!"

*One of the executives jumped up from his desk. "What do you
mean?" he asked, somewhat alarmed. "What happened?"*

*Dreyfus was holding a check in his hand and pointed to it. "I
just signed this check for a composer," he said, still excited.*

"So?" asked the other man. "How can that be a catastrophe?"

"He didn't even ask for it!" was Dreyfus's reply.

FRENCH HORNS

I have always been disappointed in the ensemble sound of the large brass section
when the French horns have been absorbed into the mass. The distinctive color
of the horns really doesn't blend with the trumpets and trombones when scored
in a tutti manner. The following example illustrates this sound:

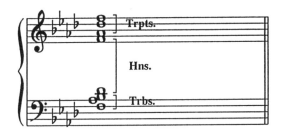

A friend and associate of mine, Charles Cassey (a very gifted arranger and
conductor), was doing an orchestration for me one time, and as I looked it over
I noticed that during a brass solo-section passage, he had placed the horns
beneath the trombones. I began to see the light. Of course, the horns in this
register have a different timbre. We all know that placing the trombones beneath
the trumpets always works well and blends well. Naturally, the horns can't go as
low as the trombones, but we can still make it work:

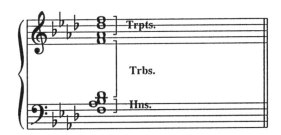

If you need to use the trombones in their low registers, then it does not make
sense to have the horns doubling them. If you need more than six voices (and don't
have a tuba for the seventh voice), then one might double all the horns an octave
below the first trumpet. If you divide them harmonically, then we're right back
where we started, with a kind of blurry sound. This example shows the horns (in
unison) doubling the melody an octave lower:

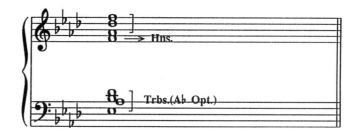

The optimum situation is to save the horns for their own type of figure—a countermelody, perhaps. In that way, they retain their own unique character and do not have to worry about attempting to blend. Horns, by the way, blend very well with low clarinets. If you only have two horns and want the homogeneity of a horn-section sound, the following example works. Note that I have dovetailed the chord:

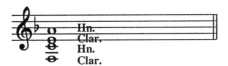

The other, more common way of treating this problem is to use two trombones with hands over the bell. The part should also be marked "quasi-horn," which will help the trombones to achieve the blend. Again, note the dovetailing:

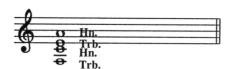

In writing for school bands, the practice has always been to double the horns with the saxophones. This has always made me uncomfortable. The reason for this approach is that the horns have historically been the weakest section in the band, and the saxes are intended to strengthen them. I usually cue the saxes when the horns are playing an important part and leave it up to the conductor's discretion. If he or she has a strong horn section, then the saxes can remain tacet, thus preserving the color of the horns. If the horn section is playing short percussive notes, then the doubling will not be so apparent.

All of the preceding discussion regarding brass blending does not apply to unison passages. Although horns have a natural affinity for unison lines with the strings, they also work well with trumpets and trombones, each section retaining its own color. Here is an example of a powerful unison line with strings:

Note that I did not use any violas in the horn line. It would be a waste, relative to the added power it would lend to the cello line. For the same reason, I kept all the violins on the top line. The horn line will benefit from the overtones of the top and bottom voices; this has always been a mystery to me but, nevertheless, it works. If your second violins are not as strong as the firsts, they could double the horns, but the firsts will lose power.

In voicing a brass section, a great deal depends on how many players you have. It doesn't take a genius to voice a chord for four trumpets and four trombones, but when you have five or six players, then a little care must be taken.

Here is an example of block writing for eight brass:

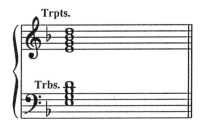

For six brass we should cover all the notes, so here is a voicing that would work just fine:

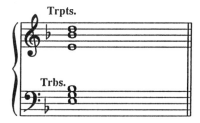

If the melody is to be doubled, then I would do it this way:

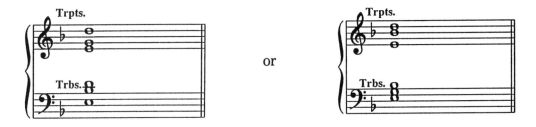

or

For a more open sound, the following works nicely:

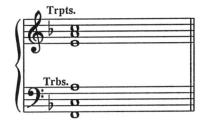

Doubling the low F an octave higher is a complete waste and won't sound as good as the previous example:

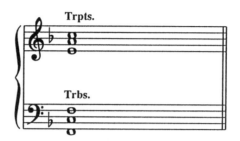

For a strong percussive note, we shall go against the norm and use closed harmony in the lower notes. Doubled with timpani, percussion and piano (an octave lower), this creates a great effect.

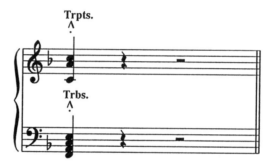

Another way of voicing this F chord is to utilize our major second. The major tonality will be destroyed, which in a case like this is not a bad thing at all:

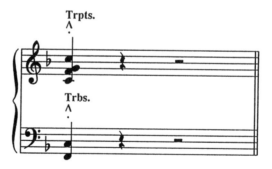

TROMBONES AND TUBA

Many of us in our arranging careers have tried in vain to get a trombone section sound out of two trombones. Using a tenor or baritone sax never really works. Sometimes, if the range is right, a flugelhorn stuck in the middle of the two may be satisfactory. Using a French horn on the bottom might be all right, but the horn must use vibrato if it's that kind of passage. Without vibrato it will be even better. The best thing to do is forget about it and make it a trombone solo or a unison duet. If the melody is adaptable to thirds, that might be a possibility, since anything sounds good in thirds except perhaps a couple of sousaphones.

When voicing three trombones and a tuba, the usual method is to place the trombones on top and the tuba at the bottom. On occasion I have felt the need for a more "biting" bottom note, and I have found that the third trombone (especially if you have a bass) can easily take the bottom part. In this case the tuba would be voiced directly above the third trombone, like this:

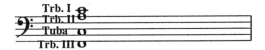

The danger, however, is that the tuba will be in a limited range. If you keep the tuba within an octave there should be no problem. I don't intend to impugn the tuba's ability to play sharp, accented notes, but sometimes I feel this blend is better with the tuba above. Also, note that the chord is complete within the trombones. The other problem becomes apparent if you do not have a bass trombone. Your bottom part won't be as flexible. If the key and ranges are right, I suggest you try it. It is, as they say in the whiskey ads, a superior blend.

I was recording a commercial in New York, and through my headphones the producer asked me if I would step into the booth.

"I don't like the oboe," he said.

"We don't have an oboe," I replied.

"What's that black pipe out there with a bulb on the end?"

"That's an English horn," I told him.

"Yeah," he replied. "It does sound a little English. I think the score should sound more continental; how about using a French horn?"

"Fine," I said. Anything to please the boss.

"One more thing," he stated. "I think it'll sound a lot better if he plays it sublissimo and not allegro."

"I'll try to remember that," I said on my way back to the studio, wondering how in the hell I ever got into this business.

After I made the revision, we played it, and he liked it very much.

"Before we make a take," he remarked, "I think tone-wise we should lower it a couple of beats."

I told him it would be a piece of cake.

Naturally, I did nothing.

THE PERCUSSION SECTION

*I*t wasn't until around the end of the eighteenth century that percussion came to be included in the symphony orchestra. The music of Vivaldi, Bach and their contemporaries contains few of these instruments. Percussion instruments were certainly used in bands and folk groups, but less often in the orchestra.

Well, a lot has changed. The battery of percussion instruments today is limitless. As a film-music composer, one is constantly aware of the need for "new sounds," and quite often one will find them in this area. The recent use of electronic drum machines is a good example. The sounds can be adjusted every which way, and the beat is always constant. Extremely fast and complex patterns that a real live drummer could never hope to duplicate, can be programmed. There are pros and cons regarding electric drums, but one has to admit that they are pretty spectacular.

Some of the percussion effects are quite unusual and can immediately create a specific mood. For example, strike a bell tree and you are transported to Indonesia or Japan. Rubbing a gong with a timpani mallet evokes an effect of the spookiest order. A snare drum pattern can suggest the military; and a timpani roll, suspense. Chimes can make music majestic or religious, and a marimba can set scenes of Spain or Mexico.

Beginning arrangers usually have a tendency to disregard drum parts, especially in the area of jazz bands. Quite often there is a single pattern with endlessly repeated measures. One is constantly learning about what percussion can and can't do and about ways to improve the writing. Years ago, I wrote a concert march called "Days of Glory" which was quite successful. It employed a repeated drum pattern (a slow British march–type beat) that gave the piece its underpinning. Here is the example:

Days of Glory

Words by
Edward Heyman

CONDENSED SCORE
Duration: 3:00

Music by
John Cacavas

If I'd known then what I know now, I'd probably have gone to a drummer and asked his or her opinion. Or, I could have messed around with it until I came up with something more effective and to-the-point. If I were going to do it again today, here is what I would do:

As you can see, I basically simplified it. By eliminating the 16th-triplet, I made it easier (especially using several drummers). By adding the extra grace notes here and there, I gave it more style. These may be small points, but nevertheless I think they'd make it a better piece.

It is becoming increasingly practical to write percussion parts in concerted form (i.e., with several parts given on each page). In this way, players can see what other section members are doing, which is extremely valuable when there is doubling. It also helps the performers to keep track of where they are. It is easier to count measures when one can watch what's happening in the other parts.

I usually put the snare drum, bass drum and cymbals (both struck and hand-held) on one part. If the timpani part is not too busy, I'll include bells and chimes along with it (on a separate staff, of course). All the others will go on a separate part. I do not recommend using a three-staff percussion part because it becomes too unwieldy.

If there are long periods of inactivity, I will give a four-bar instrumental cue preceding the percussionists' entry. This prevents an awful lot of misplaced gong crashes, believe me. Say, for example, that a timpanist has 32 measures of rests before entering. I would place one cue on measure 12, and another one at measure 28. This type of cueing is especially valuable when the music contains meter changes and rubatos. Again, I return to the same point: if it makes for ease of performance and a reduced chance for mistakes, do it. Always put yourself in the performer's place.

In jazz-band drum parts, more is better. Designate right there on the part who is playing. It gives the player more leeway in varying what he or she might do. You might want to include certain figures, such as brass licks. Don't make the mistake of leaving out dynamic indications. The percussionist is as much of a musician as anyone else. Although professionals are truly whizzes, give the players time to switch from mallets to sticks, or to brushes. This can be difficult, but the drummer can play with one hand if necessary while making these adjustments.

> *There's a story in Hollywood about a particular no-talent conductor-arranger who was rehearsing a piece in a recording studio. The music was so terrible and so filled with mistakes that the musicians just looked mournfully at one another. It was obvious that the conductor didn't even know how bad everything was.*
>
> *Finally the timpanist could take it no longer. As loudly as he could, he let loose with a series of "thumpity-thump-thump-thump-thumps," which stopped the rehearsal.*
>
> *The conductor looked up from his score and said, "All right, who did that?"*

Here are a few percussion hints:

1. Remember, the bells (or glockenspiel) sound two octaves higher than written. Be sure to designate the kind of mallets you want. The hard ones sound strident; I prefer the softer ones, which give you more tone.

2. Unless otherwise told, the vibraphonist's motor will be running, which will give you a vibrato. This is fine for shimmering effects, but state "motor off" if you want a sound that will blend with flutes, piano and so forth.

3. When you mark a snare drum "muffled," many players will take off the snares, which will make the drum sound like a tom-tom. Tell them (or mark it on the part) to put a billfold at the edge of the drum. This will give you the proper sound.

4. If you want a cymbal roll to sound right, make sure you indicate "soft mallets" or, better yet, "softest mallets." Otherwise, the player might use sticks.

5. Remember, there are triangles of various sizes. If you want a deeper sound, write "large triangle," and vice versa for a very light effect.

6. When you want a cymbal crash, be exact. Do you want two cymbals struck together, or just one struck with a mallet or stick? Mark the part accordingly.

7. How do you want the bass drum to sound on, for example, a march? Tight? Booming? Whatever you're after, mark it on the part so the player can adjust the drum as to your liking.

8. Be careful of the xylophone. Like the piccolo, it can cut through a large orchestra. It also sounds an octave higher than written. This instrument can be very effective for playing short, staccato passages with high woodwinds and brass—but don't overdo it.

9. How much time does it take for the timpanist to change the pitch? It's always been a mystery to me how a timpanist can change pitches while the rest of the ensemble is going full blast. Before the piece, it's easy. All he or she does is make the settings. During a performance, a change is often only a step up or down, which is not too difficult. If in doubt, speak to the player and get a quick refresher course.

10. If more than one snare drum is to play a pattern, make sure the part says so.

11. In the areas of jazz and rock bands, a good drummer can often come up with something better than what you've written. I often write out the pattern but append a little note saying, "or your own." I'm never disappointed.

12. The vibraphone and marimba have very poor carrying power. Unless the orchestration is extremely transparent these instruments may not be heard. Consider using some amplification if it is available.

13. Don't make the mistake of writing the chimes out of range. Most instruments can move between middle C and the F that's an octave and a fourth higher. Some of the newer models can go a tone higher, to G.

14. In most of the standard repertoire, a cymbal crash is designated like this: ⨯. To me, this is ambiguous. Is it meant to ring out or be short? If I want it to ring out, I do it this way: ⨯⌒. This is also applicable to gongs. Some composers have used a whole note for a ringing effect, but I find that unsatisfactory. If the hand is used to dampen it, I think the effect is lost.

The usual setup for the timpani calls for four drums. Here are their ranges, beginning with the lowest drum:

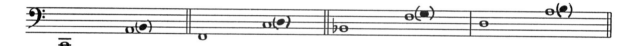

I don't think I have ever used the top drum, since I have always conceived of this instrument in terms of its lower reaches. Although these drums may vary about two or three inches in size (depending upon the manufacturer), the tones are the same for all practical purposes.

It is certainly possible for the player to play on two drums at the same time. This is particularly effective with fifths in a heavily accented pattern. For a clearer effect with two drums, octaves are quite effective.

Although the new instruments are equipped with pedal tuning devices, many are still around that must be tuned by the original tension screws. Obviously this makes tuning during a performance more difficult.

For a great "thud" effect, hit the drum smack in the center with hard mallets.

The timpanist has many mallets to choose from. If you're not sure what you want, just indicate on the part the effect that you wish. The player will then be able to make the proper decision. I usually ask for either hard or regular mallets.

In 1967 the New York Public Library was sponsoring a retrospective of the works of Ira Gershwin that was being set up by Chappell. I hadn't seen Ira in a few months, although we had been corresponding quite frequently, especially about his writing lyrics to the unpublished Kern songs. (At the time, I was director of publications for the company.)

I was happy that he and his wife decided to come to New York for the event and was looking forward to seeing him. The day he arrived he called me from the Regency Hotel where he was staying. He asked if I was free at around 2:30 that afternoon, and I assured him that if I wasn't, I would cancel any appointment that I had. After all, it wasn't just any day that Ira Gershwin came to the office. He was brought into my office, and at once I realized from the expression on his face that all was not well. He sat down on the sofa. As he looked around my office, I wondered how the drawings and paintings adorning my walls (created by my small children) stacked up to his Picassos and Modiglianis.

"I understand you're upset with my wife, Lee," he said. Of course I was upset with his wife. She had been trying to undermine my efforts to get Ira back to writing lyrics ever since I met him. But why would he bring this up? Obviously, I must have mentioned it to somebody, and it got back to him. I hoped this wasn't his sole reason for coming up to see me.

"Let's just say I don't understand her," I said to him. "You must admit that she's been rather rude to me every time I've come to see you."

He remained silent.

"There's nothing personal in my feeling," I continued, "and if I've offended you or her, for that I'm sorry. But I'm not sorry for encouraging you to write again."

It was a very tense moment, and I waited for him to say something.

"Do you mind if I have a cigar?" he said.

Feeling a small amount of relief I said, "Please feel free to light up."

With that he pulled out a huge cigar, the kind that Winston Churchill smoked. He lit it, and soon the office was filled with clouds of smoke. He puffed in contented silence for a few moments.

"I hope that wasn't your reason for coming to see me," I said.

"No, no, that wasn't it at all," he replied. "It's really a little embarrassing. You know how I enjoy a good cigar."

I nodded.

"Well, Lee and I have a suite over at the Regency, and she doesn't want me to smoke in there. Smells up the rooms, she says. . . . I would feel a little self-conscious sitting in the lobby, so I thought about you. All I want is to sit down, have a good cigar and maybe talk about our songs. By the way, would you like a cigar?"

I hated the things; I never smoked them. "Of course," I said. "There's nothing better than a good cigar. Should I order some coffee?"

He smiled contentedly and took another huge drag.

An example of percussion effects is shown in the introduction of my symphonic band arrangement of John Williams's *E.T., The Extra-Terrestrial.* Using the vibes was my way of substituting the violin section's ethereal "sweeps." The gongs and cymbals I took from his score, but using the arms on the piano was my idea. The combination of these three instruments created the ghostly effect that I was after. Since the only instruments playing against this combination were the woodwinds, I was confident that the sound of these instruments would come through.

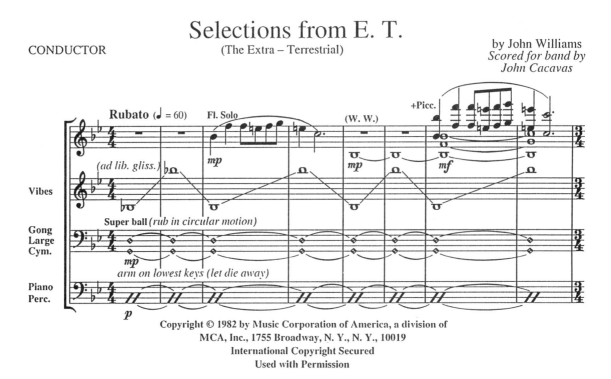

Selections from E. T.

(The Extra – Terrestrial)

CONDUCTOR

by John Williams
Scored for band by
John Cacavas

In recent years the use of percussion in marching bands has become quite varied. The use of tuned tom-toms is employed extensively in what is called "corps" style. If you are going to do this type of writing, it is best to find out what is going to be available to you. Below are two examples of this kind of drum arranging.

I

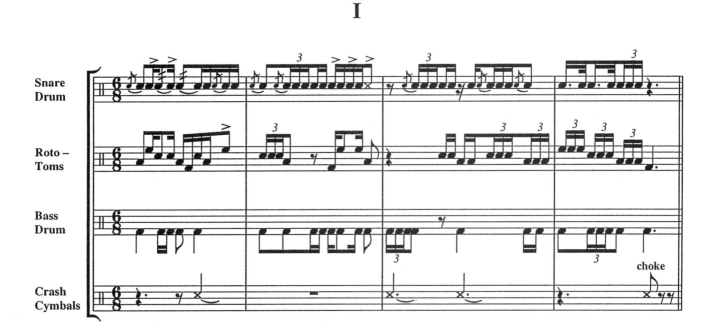

II

I have always been interested in seeking out new percussion sounds. In Los Angeles, many of the instrument rental agencies have all kinds of different instruments available, which offers a great opportunity to try out all these things.

Percussion instruments from the exotic East are always fascinating, although their use is limited.

Today the synthesizer is capable of reproducing some of these sounds extremely well. Not only that, they can be preprogrammed, and their sound will always be consistent.

I recall doing a Dracula movie in England one time and needing something called a "water chime." The contractor notified one of the percussionists, who showed up with a gong and a pail, which he filled with water. The gong was struck and then quickly dipped into the pail. This created a long descent in pitch that was really spooky. Nowadays there is a special device that holds several different-sized gongs and automatically drops them into a trough of water. However, you can still do it the old-fashioned way, which works fine.

One last thought: give your players a map. Don't write out 48 1/4 measures of rest and then ask for an important cymbal crash. Let the player know what's happening among the other parts so the entrance will always be correct.

A couple of very young studio executives had just been notified that the director of an upcoming picture for their studio wanted the music of Mozart for the project.

As one of the execs hung up the phone, he asked the other: "Is he any good?"

The other guy shrugged his shoulders. "Must be if the director wants him. He's very knowledgeable about music."

The first executive thought for a moment. "Well, get on with it. Find out who Mozart's agent is so we can make a deal."

THE STRING SECTION

*T*he string section is probably the most versatile of all the instrument families. Their range is tremendous, their articulation is limitless, and they never run out of breath. Besides their regular sounds, they are capable of many effects including pizzicato, harmonics and many others. When they are muted they produce a silky, veiled effect, and when played with the back of the bow they become quite percussive.

They are blessed with the ability to project great warmth, but they can also turn right around and be very sinister and foreboding. Who can forget the shark theme in *Jaws*?

Their agility is one of their greatest characteristics. Only the woodwinds can come close to imitating their rapid articulation—but then after a while even they will run out of steam. It is no coincidence that this family of instruments has become the backbone of classical repertoire and probably the most important section of the symphony orchestra.

I have found many orchestration books quite wanting in the various suggestions for string harmonization that they offer. It seems that the examples of structure they provide run contrary to what I (and many of my colleagues) have learned regarding string voicing. It is also interesting to note that what works well for strings does not necessarily work well for the wind or brass family. One of the reasons for this, I believe, is the overtones created by the strings.

A great deal of how you are going to treat your strings depends on how many you have. You certainly have limitations when you are writing for five violins, a viola and a cello rather than a full symphonic section.

One of the biggest errors that I see in string writing is the tendency to divide too much and too often. Look at any symphony by Tchaikovsky and you will see unisons, unisons in three octaves and open harmony. Maurice Ravel, a master of orchestration, goes many steps farther, using special effects and so forth, but still handles the strings masterfully.

Stravinsky's writing seems to go in another direction that *does* involve a lot of divisi, but the end justifies the means in his case.

In the Baroque period the orchestration of strings was simple. All one needs to do is examine the works of Vivaldi to see that the basses usually doubled the cellos an octave lower, and the violins usually played in close three-part harmony and sometimes in thirds. In many cases the violas supplied the third note in the chord. One must also bear in mind that orchestras were smaller in those days. Most of the works of the period had a keyboard part that covered all the bases in case Franz, Max or Josef didn't show up for the performance. In other words, the golden age of orchestration was yet to come.

Elsewhere in this book, I have touched upon devices that pertain to the strings, but I will now give examples of my experience that I hope will be illuminating.

HARMONY

To create a lush, open sound, I will give an example that goes against most harmony books. The top voices are open, and the bottom ones are closed. This gives a huge sound and conveys an aura of spaciousness.

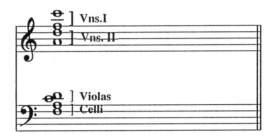

The works of Tchaikovsky are abundant with various examples of open-harmony string writing. The two examples below show a typical example in four-part harmony and the same kind of voicing with only three-part harmony. Note that only the root and fifth are doubled.

Symphony Pathètique

I

II

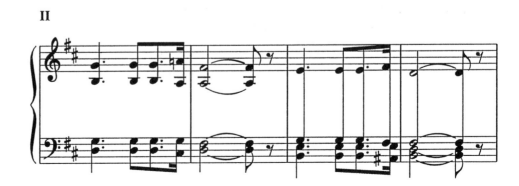

Another voicing of incredible lushness utilizes three-part harmony with an octave between the two top voices. The secret to the sound is adhering to the three parts and not cluttering them up with a fourth voice. I have used the four-part harmony on occasion, but it seems a little muddled and not as clear as three parts.

Another version of this voicing would involve dropping the bottom two voices. This would result in the melody being presented in three octaves. The sound is quite wonderful and would be practical if the string section were smaller than in the previous example.

What makes the sound of this string setting unique are the two high octaves without any harmony in between. The application of this voicing in arranging music of a light nature, such as theater or film music, is very effective. Unfortunately, it does not work too well with a limited section. On one occasion when I was faced with that problem, I had just one violin on the second voice and doubled it with two flutes. It wasn't too bad.

The use of thirds in string writing is always effective. An example follows:

If you have a bigger section, the thirds can be doubled an octave lower:

If you have a large section and the range permits, string instruments can be doubled another octave lower. This creates a huge sonorous effect that is very brilliant indeed:

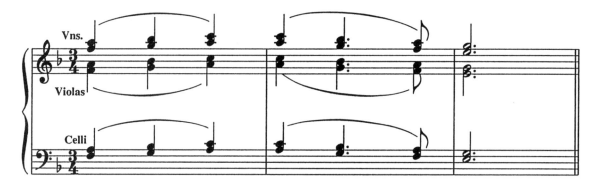

To help strengthen the sound, woodwinds can be interspersed if desired. For a total tutti effect that includes trumpets, this example works very well.

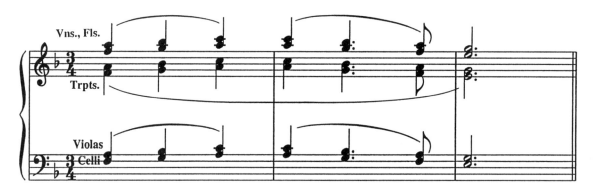

The use of thirds in two octaves is demonstrated in Tchaikovsky's "Waltz of the Flowers" from the *Nutcracker Suite*. Note that in measures 5 and 6, the strings are not playing the third; it is in the bass. Not only that, but you won't find the third in the horn afterbeats either. If you are familiar with the work, you know how this section really sings out at you.

My fondness for open string writing does not mean that I categorically dismiss closed writing. On the contrary, there are certain kinds of passages that require a tight kind of sound, especially when the strings play a background figure, or the tessitura of the situation prevents a full-blown approach. Delicate or soft material will sometimes dictate this style, as the following example, again from Tchaikovsky's *Nutcracker Suite*, shows:

Note that it is marked *pp* and that the orchestration is unique. The "seconds" of the violin IIs come in only a couple of times to complete the chord. Same thing with the violas. It was obviously scored in this manner for purposes of balance.

Certain melodies lend themselves to scoring in open sixths. Although they're less flexible than thirds, it's still a good sound. Because of the spread, one could not use the triple-octave voicing that we used with the thirds.

In pizzicato treatments, I tend to avoid placing the strings in closed harmony. Compared to open harmony, closed harmony gets to be too tight. The following example "opens up" to a much better sound.

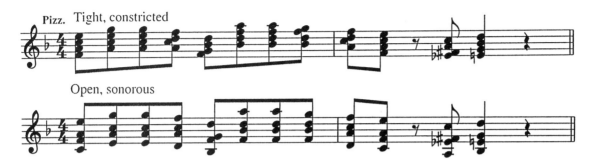

Pizz. Tight, constricted

Open, sonorous

The next example opens the chords even farther with the addition of the melody an octave lower for strength. Because of the high placement, putting the melody on the top octave only would be too thin. All these open voicings described thus far would also sound excellent played arco.

One should not think of strings as always playing concerted or as a section. They are actually an orchestra unto themselves, divided into four sections: the violins (I and II), the violas, the cellos and the basses. When writing for them in a contrapuntal manner, one can strengthen the weak sections by judiciously using the woodwinds—bassoons with cellos, for example, or clarinets with violas. It seems that more often than not we are faced with a smaller string section than we'd like. An example of this kind of divided-section writing is something like this:

Montage for Strings

FULL SCORE

John Cacavas

Another version of this style of string treatment is as follows:

The Day the Orchestra Played
A Fantasy for Narrator and Orchestra

Text and Narration by
Charles O. Wood

Music by
John Cacavas

Jan Ericksen, one of the top music producers for the Norwegian Radio Broadcasting System, told me a story worth repeating.

Sir Malcolm Sargent, the British conductor, was rehearsing a program with the London Symphony, and time was running out. Among the works for performance that evening was the Brahms Second Symphony. Knowing that the piece was a very familiar one, he asked the orchestra if they might just pass on it.

As they were preparing to move on to the next piece, the second oboe player raised his hand.

"Maestro," he said, "I've never played this work before."

"You'll love it," was the reply.

Earlier we mentioned the possibility of adding woodwinds to the strings to create certain effects. In the previous piece, *The Day the Orchestra Played*, the opening was a strong brass tutti fanfare that needed the extra power of high woodwinds along with strings. Note that it is scored with open harmony. If I were to rescore this example, I would most likely have added the cellos to the rest of the strings, or at least divided them—half with the low C, the others playing the first violin part down two octaves. (The tuba and bass trombone were also on the low pedal C.)

TREMOLO

The use of tremolo, if not overdone, can provide a variety of special effects. It can impart an aura of *misterioso* or danger and, with certain kinds of chords, a sense of openness or grandeur. Basically there are two kinds of tremolo: the first, in which the strings play the same note with very rapid bowing; the other, in which the strings go from one note to another, creating a sort of harmony from the intervals, so to speak. This could be an exception to my usual avoidance of high strings in closed harmony, especially when a thin sound is desired. Here is an example:

By placing three beams on the quarter-notes we approximate 32nd-notes. If we used two beams, we would have 16th-notes and so on.

The other effect is used more often for conveying grandeur, nature and openness. Here is that example:

Another way to create more excitement with this device is to have some of the strings play a trill. If the section is small, however, woodwinds could take over this function. Here is an example:

In the previous two examples, it appears that the third note in the chord, D, would move to the same note in the next chord. Here is a way around it:

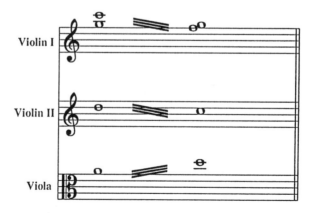

Low strings, either in unison or in simple harmony, can create an effect of ominousness. Just remember that the basses cannot move around as fast as the cellos. In high string tremolos, using mutes can create a glassy sound, just as bowing techniques will impart a thin sound in that register. Again, as with many effects, do not do it too much, or the effectiveness will be lost. In all the previous examples note that the strings are in their higher registers. If they go too low, this effect tends to become muddled and thick (unless you want a dark, harsh sound). As a matter of fact, you hear a lot of low, accented tremolos in Dracula movies! Just remember that low tremolos will not sound like a spring morning while at the seaside.

HARMONICS

Again, this is a device that, if not overdone, can be very useful. The sound produced is thin, eerie and glassy. Natural harmonics can be played on the open strings and are designated like this:

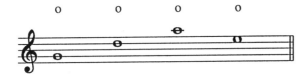

Other harmonics, called artificial harmonics, have a diamond-shaped note placed a fourth above the note, which will create a sound two octaves higher (an accidental need not be placed on the diamond-shaped note). An example follows:

By the way, don't use mutes when you are writing harmonics.

OTHER DEVICES

"Ponticello" (meaning "by the bridge") imparts a thin, glassy sound and is good for ethereal passages.

"Sul tasto" means bowing over the fingerboard, which provides a thin nasal quality.

"Détaché" signifies the use of "long bows," which means pulling as much as possible throughout the duration of a note:

"Spiccato" means bouncing the bow on the string for a light, fast staccato:

"Col legno" designates bowing with the wooden side of the bow, best used for active rhythms:

"Portamento" means having the strings slide to another note, and is designated thus:

DOUBLE-STOPS

This is an area best approached with a great deal of thought. Just because a stringed instrument can play two or three notes at the same time doesn't mean that it always works. This device is most effective with accented notes that do not move quickly. Three-note chords are not as accurate because of the curvature of the string bridge. When played, they will sound slightly arpeggiated. Playing a moving passage entirely composed of double-stops is not practical and should be avoided. Large chords with space in between is your best bet. Remember that the notes you wish to use as double-stops cannot be on the same string. And remember never to write them for the string bass. Fifths, sixths and sevenths (with certain octaves) are your best bet.

Double-stopping should not be employed in a continuous manner unless it is simplified, as in the following example:

The next example would be awkward and difficult:

I remember one occasion on which I thought I was going to have a much larger string section than I ended up with. Because some of the parts were marked "divisi," I just told the string players to use double-stops whenever it was convenient—especially on whole notes during slow tempos.

There are several books on the market that discuss double-stops in detail. It's worth it to have one in your library.

An example of fortissimo double-stops can be found at the end of the first section of Beethoven's Fifth Symphony. Note that the second violin has a triple-stop. It will not sound exactly on the beat but will be slightly arpeggiated instead. (The abbreviation "Br." is the term for "Bratsche," or viola, in German.)

Rather large chords comprising quadruple-stops appear later in the work. Again, they are played fortissimo. Less able players could probably divide them up into groups of double-stops.

BOWINGS

As a rule, I do not provide bowings for the strings. I much prefer to mark in the phrasing that I desire and leave it up to the player from there. I have written a lot of arrangements for symphony orchestra that I perform on pops concerts from time to time. I am continually amazed that when I examine the string parts after a performance, I notice the bowings have been altered from previous performances.

So I simply elect to exclude myself from an area that is so fraught with subjectiveness. In other words, it seems to be something that nobody agrees upon, so I don't want to be the referee.

The exception to the rule is publications or works intended for very young players. Unless you are a string player or have an extensive knowledge of bowing techniques, this aspect of your writing is best left to an expert. On the few occasions that I have written something for a young orchestra, I have farmed out the bowing. To reiterate my stance, I don't think you'll go wrong by marking the phrasing just the way you want it. Often an orchestra instructor will change what you've done anyway. If you want to mark in the bowings entirely (and are not that familiar with the craft), just get some help. Nothing wrong with that.

A Hollywood composer-conductor who was quite a lightweight in the talent department wanted to impress his producer with his musical prowess. Before the session he would write a mistake into the first trumpet part (for example, a C-natural instead of a C-sharp).

When he got to that spot during rehearsal, he would immediately stop the orchestra and tell the trumpet player to play C-sharp.

"In bar 40, you played a C-natural," he said. "Play C-sharp!"

"I played the right note," said the trumpet player. "Before the session I went through my parts, found the mistake and fixed it."

The orchestra suppressed their giggles. I don't know about the producer.

CHORAL MUSIC

Writing for choral publication is a very broad and lucrative area that is divided into two main categories—sacred writing and secular writing. Both arrangements of classical pieces and originals have a broad market. In the sacred sector, the Bible is a fine source for texts. In the secular area, you have the option of arranging songs from the public domain, especially those of the old masters. Then you have the pop or novelty area. Recent years have brought another category to light: the combining of religious and pop choral composition. This is highly specialized but is becoming increasingly popular as church services (in certain denominations) are mixing these two idioms.

To write in this field, a lot of research must be done. First, as with instrumental music, check with a music dealer to find out both what and who is hot. A visit to your local church or school choir will also be an invaluable aid.

The main categories in all choral writing are SATB, SSA, SA, SAB and TTBB.

If it is a secular choral piece, you'll have to write a piano part. If it is pop, you may consider an optional rhythm section. For church music, the organ will replace the piano. For more ambitious works, sometimes brass and timpani are added.

You must also select a grade of difficulty. Obviously you can write more difficult music for a mixed choir (SATB) than for a young girls' chorus of SSA parts. In many cases, if an SATB piece is successful, the publisher asks the arranger to score it for SSA, SAB and so on.

In the area of serious secular music, there is a great untapped wealth of material in old folk songs of various nationalities. One can find much of this music in collections and music libraries. Furthermore, all you have to do is translate the original language for your text. Chances are you'll already have your piano part, which may only need a little simplification.

Arrangements of famous folk songs have been done to death, but that doesn't mean that a wonderful, fresh setting of "Danny Boy" or "Annie Laurie" might not be a hit.

There are two ways of scoring SATB. One is the open system, the other is the closed. The advantage of the open system is that it's easier for the performers to read. The disadvantage, and this is strictly from the publisher's point of view, is that it's more expensive to print because the systems are larger. Here are examples:

Open System

In the open system, the tenor is written in treble clef but actually sounds an octave lower.

Closed System

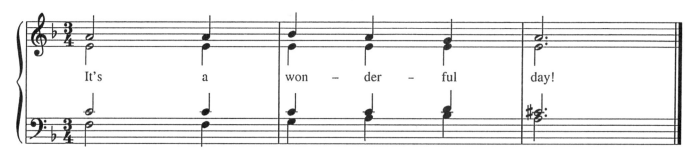

The big difference here, in the closed system, is that the tenor now must read in bass clef, and the music will sound exactly as it is written. Sometimes the publisher will have the words placed below the bass part (in addition to the middle of the system). One should also remember that the piano or organ part will be directly below the systems. In typical octavo-size parts, the closed system will contain four units per page, whereas the open system will have two. My advice is to score the work in closed system first, as this makes it easier for a prospective publisher to peruse it. If necessary, you can then rescore it the other way.

In works of an *a capella* nature (i.e., with no accompaniment), you should always have the choral parts (in small notes) duplicated in closed system on a separate piano staff if the work is scored in open system. This is necessary for rehearsal. However, you need not do this if your piece is being printed in closed system, since the pianist can read directly from the choral parts.

Be careful with ranges. Writing for immature voices restricts the flexibility you'd have with a high school, college or adult church choir.

Voice-leading is far more critical in choral writing than it is in instrumental writing. Whereas most instruments can count on a tone being sounded when they press a key, a singer has to replicate the note in his or her head and try to reproduce it.

Certain jumps—tritones (augmented fourths), augmented fifths and major sevenths—are very difficult and should be avoided if possible. If a tritone is in the melody, however, it is not so difficult.

When writing anything dissonant for a choir, remember that without tonality, there will be no frame of reference for the singers. Major and minor chords are ingrained in the musical memory of a singer, and the proper reproduction of these chords comes from their prior experience. With atonal material there is no such reference. Try to ease into it as easily as possible, be it via a unison or simple chord. Getting into the dissonant chords using stepwise motion will save a lot of headaches and rehearsal time.

Be very careful of writing an extended *a capella* section and then entering the piano or an instrumental accompaniment. More than likely, the chorus will have drifted off pitch slightly, and when the instruments or piano come in, the disparity might be a little jarring. If the new section is in a different key, it won't be quite as bad. One way around this problem is to let a little time elapse before coming in after the *a capella*. The previous tonality will have died away somewhat, and if the singers have "drifted" it won't be quite so noticeable.

When you are scoring for voices be sure to take into account the problems of breathing and phrasing. Singers, like wind-instrument players, have limited breathing capacity, so bear that in mind. For purposes of practicality, I like to place a comma at the point where I wish a breath to be taken. If you have a long phrase you might mark the parts "stagger breathing," which means that you will end up with a continuous phrase. This works best in unisons, obviously.

There is another technique that means "take it in one breath," if possible. It is a broken phrase line and looks like this:

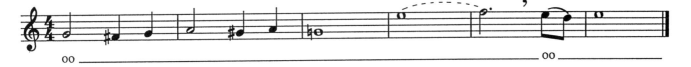

Today, choral or group voice parts for contemporary pop music are very simple, utilizing harmony in three parts at the most and two parts quite often. Unison and open fifths are quite popular in rock music.

The close, tight harmony of the 1940s and 1950s is not much in vogue anymore, but it is wonderful when performed well. The harmonic alterations and structure of the Hi-Lo's for example, was quite a treat. Later years have brought us groups like Singers Unlimited and Manhattan Transfer, which are continuing the tradition. You will hardly ever hear a root in these groups' chords, by the way. The intonation must be right on the money because of the many half-steps in the harmony. If you listen to any of these recordings, you will note the lack of vibrato. The songs are all sung very "straight" in order for the harmonies to come through.

It's a good idea to avoid hard syllables on long notes. To hold four slow beats of "ee" is not too pleasant. The same goes for "I." Whenever possible, use "soft" syllables for your long notes.

After you've written your voice parts, sing them over to yourself. You will then notice the weaknesses and be able to correct them. As with instrumental music, put yourself in the shoes of the performer.

The following episode took place during one of my periodic visits to London while I was with Chappell.

Richard Rodgers and Irving Berlin would periodically come to London on a combined mission of business and pleasure. Williamson Music, Inc. (Rodgers and Hammerstein's company) and Irving Berlin Music Ltd. were both located on the ground floor in one of the Chappell buildings. Both Rodgers and Berlin assumed they each had a separate office, but that was not the case. They shared an office with two interchangeable brass nameplates in front of the door. Whenever one or the other would arrive in London, the pictures on the walls would be replaced, as well as the sheet music and catalogs that were placed around the office. Naturally, the offending front-door brass plate would also be removed and the correct one substituted. This went on for years with neither one of them ever suspecting.

As luck would have it, an occasion arose when both men were visiting London. Rodgers was supposed to arrive around 11:00 in the morning, and suddenly the staff received a call that Berlin was coming in about noon. It became apparent to all that a catastrophe was in the making. Since there was not that much to do in the office, everyone figured that Rodgers would mosey around a bit, then go upstairs to meet with Louis Dreyfus, the chairman of Chappell. Unfortunately, he puttered around a little too long, and it soon became dangerously close to noon. Finally, somebody had the bright idea of telling Rodgers that Mr. Dreyfus had arrived, and could he please join him upstairs. As soon as Rodgers left, the staff frantically replaced pictures and sheet music and other telltale bits of evidence. The nameplate was hastily changed—and not a moment too soon, for at the stroke of noon in walked Irving Berlin to view his offices.

For the next few days it was touch-and-go as various employees maintained a close vigil and made frantic changes. Fortunately, Berlin went off to the Continent, so things returned to normal. It was never determined whether or not Dreyfus learned of these machinations—but it was probably true that the office rents were not split down the middle.

ELECTRONIC APPLICATIONS IN ORCHESTRATION

*E*lectronic and synthesized effects have become an extremely important and viable presence in our music. As composers and arrangers, we are faced with an astounding array of keyboards, computers, drum machines and other instruments. To complicate matters further, what is popular and usable today can become obsolete tomorrow with the technological advances being made.

As a composer and arranger for films, I use synthesizers constantly. However, I write what I want and leave it to the performers that I hire to implement it for me. This means lots of discussions about sounds and effects and the various approaches that I wish to take. What I really do is leave it up to the performers and programmers to give me what I want. If I do not achieve the effect I want, especially on the scoring stage, we just search until we find it.

Because I am basically interested in just writing music, I decided to ask an expert to write this much-needed chapter on electronic music.

I first met Steve Kaplan when he was very young and just starting out as a demo player in Hollywood. I was very impressed with his talent and especially his ability to come up in short order with sounds that I wanted. I began to use him for my films, and very soon he became one of the most sought-after studio musicians in Hollywood. His credits are quite impressive. In feature motion pictures he performed on the sound tracks of *Terms of Endearment, Easy Money, The Toy, Flight of the Intruder, Dutch* and many others. His television performances have included "Murder She Wrote," "Matlock," "The Young and the Restless," "Hill Street Blues," "Knots Landing," "Cheers," "The Simpsons," "The Equalizer" and hundreds of others. As a composer, he has written many sequences for a variety of television movies. He has also been a featured keyboard artist on most of the country's major record labels.

I think Steve has given me exactly what I asked for regarding this exciting and extremely complex medium. It is informative and practical and will be of immense help to anyone who is in the business of writing music.

Whenever I go to one of my sessions and see Steve with his huge rack of keyboards, computers and blinking lights, I swear that I might be lifted off into space with all those machines. I may not go to the moon, but I am always uplifted when I hear the magnificent sounds those machines can create.

ELECTRONIC APPLICATIONS IN ORCHESTRATION

by Steve Kaplan

In the last twenty years, we have seen incredible changes in the music world, due in no small part to the introduction of synthesizers and electronic instruments. For hundreds of years, man's ears have been used to hearing certain sounds within a musical framework. Woodwinds, brass, percussion and stringed instruments have been around for centuries, long enough for us to become accustomed to their tonal colors. But as recently as thirty years ago, virtually none of us had heard music incorporating electronic sounds (although such pieces certainly existed in avant garde circles). It is indicative of a pretty radical shift that today, in the 1990s, you cannot turn on the radio (not to mention MTV) without hearing synthesized music of some kind or another.

We are talking about a relatively new form of musical expression, an evolving art form in which exploration and experimentation are helping us to discover uses that are applicable to music. And the technology is moving forward at such an exponential rate that new instruments (e.g., synthesizers) can become obsolete almost from the moment they become available to us.

What is clear is that since the introduction of the early synthesizers in the 1960s (utilized in the groundbreaking work of Walter Carlos's *Switched on Bach*, 1968) we have learned a tremendous amount about the musical capabilities and limitations of electronics in music. For one thing, our instruments today have quite a bit more range and flexibility than they did back then. Certain sounds that used to be technically difficult or downright impossible to reproduce are now taken for granted as standard presets in the simplest synths. Since that earlier time, we have learned what synthesizers can and cannot do well. This is still an extremely young field, and both the technology and our knowledge of how to apply it continues to grow at a mind-boggling rate.

I became interested in synthesizers in college in the mid-1970s. I had been a classically trained pianist as a kid, in addition to having a great interest in jazz and rock. But I started to hear more and more electronic textures on the records I was listening to, and I decided to take the plunge and buy a synthesizer. I went down to my local music store and bought an ARP Axxe, the cheapest monophonic (one-voice) synth available at the time. To say that the Axxe was limited and archaic as an instrument is to understate the case, but for a kid with no experience in these sonic worlds, it was nirvana. As time went on and synthesizer technology progressed, I continued to keep up with the latest keyboards and devices, and over the years I have spent hundreds of thousands of dollars on these magical (and expensive!) toys. I will admit to being slightly fanatical about the subject, and I don't necessarily suggest that the reader will need to invest huge amounts of money or time in order to become familiar with the world of electronic music. I will say, though, that for a person with a certain predilection, this can be an addictive (and rewarding) area of study.

For a composer or orchestrator, synthesizers, drum machines and so on present certain specific issues that are very different from those aspects pertaining to performers of electronic music. A composer should be familiar with the range of textures within the synthesizer family and should know how to write effectively for the instruments, but it is not necessary for him or her to be a virtuoso player or programmer. Needless to say, a composer who plays trumpet, for example, will usually be able to write a trumpet part that lies well on that particular horn. Likewise, a composer with a fair amount of experience with synths will write idiomatically for those instruments' various sounds. This is all to say that a little knowledge about synths cannot possibly hurt you, and the more you know, the more effectively you will be able to approach the instruments compositionally.

Another issue pertaining specifically to the composer is the incorporation of electronics into the orchestral environment. If a synth part is written properly, it will support the orchestra without overwhelming it. If a synth is to be featured at a certain point in a piece, it is important to orchestrate in such a way that the sound can cut through and be heard effectively. As you become more familiar with synth sounds, you begin to notice a fundamental difference in the character of an analog or digital color and the sound of an acoustic instrument. You have to adjust accordingly for these differences. Just as a composer or orchestrator must be able to communicate with the players through a musical vocabulary of terms, in the same way you must be at least somewhat aware of the terminology of electronic music. Believe me, it will save you a lot of headaches. In mapping out a part, you should give clear indications as to what kind of sound you want to hear. If possible, it is best not to overwrite or to force your synthesist to make impossible sound switches in an unreasonably short period of time. If the part is playable, your synthesist will be able to devote a larger part of his or her attention to refining the quality of the sound (which is a high priority), which will reduce the time spent trying to navigate a sea of technical difficulties.

GETTING FAMILIAR CONTROLLERS

It's a good idea to know a little bit about the types of instruments available to you. To start, let's break down the basic types of synth controllers there are to choose from. A controller is simply the type of instrument you are using to produce your synth sound. In the synthesizer world, not all instruments are keyboard-based; there are different controllers for different musical applications. There are horn and woodwind synths (also known as EVI and EWI for short), percussion devices (drum machines and live drum controllers), mallet-based controllers for vibraphonists, synths controlled by guitar or bass, and others that I'm sure are being developed even as I write this. Recently, I heard from a violinist that a violin-based synth controller was in development, but I cannot personally vouch for the accuracy of this report. The same synth sounds can be played (or triggered) by any type of controller. However, certain sounds are easier to play expressively when triggered by a specific controller.

Generally speaking, you will tend to see more keyboard controller synths around than anything else. The keyboard is ideal for producing a polyphonic (or chordal) texture. When you are writing for one to simulate a string section, or one that requires several notes being played at once, the keyboard controller is the best choice.

When writing for a solo type of sound, the horn synths are very effective. The EVI is a brass synth (with brass fingerings) and the EWI is a woodwind synth (with reed fingerings). These are monophonic synthesizers, and sound is produced by the player blowing into the instrument, just as with a horn or woodwind instrument. The breath offers a high level of control for such features as vibrato, which makes the horn synth very expressive and ideal for solo applications. However, writing chordal parts for your EVI player will be more difficult.

Percussion controllers are set up to be struck with sticks or mallets. There are mallet controllers that are configured in the form of vibes or xylophone. Drum controllers are generally configured in the form of a drum kit, and the player strikes various pads to produce the sounds. Guitar and bass guitar synth controllers are played from guitars and basses, respectively. When properly applied, the guitar synth can create some stunning effects (e.g., when strumming a chord), and doubling your bass part with a synth bass sound can really help fatten up the bottom of your arrangement.

SOUND MODULES

Now that you know a little bit about controllers, you're probably wondering what those instruments are controlling. We live in a rapidly miniaturizing world. We are making devices that are a fraction of the size of older devices while being many times more powerful. Twenty years ago (the Stone Age from a synthesist's viewpoint), a Moog modular synthesizer took up the space of half a room, and required extensive patching to achieve the desired results. Today, we have synths that can create similar results in the size of a small keyboard or *sound module*.

Quite simply, a sound module is a synthesizer, usually in the shape of a rectangular metallic box, but without a controlling device (e.g., keyboard). Back in the early days, almost all keyboard synths had sound modules built into the same unit. You plugged your vintage Prophet 5 synthesizer into an amplifier and you were ready to go. The keyboard and the sound module were one unit. But today, you can have one keyboard controller that drives dozens of disembodied sound modules all at once. This can be an extremely efficient use of space, since you can stack your sound modules in a rack, one on top of another, playing them all simultaneously from your keyboard, and literally have an electronic orchestra in your house or studio. EVIs, percussion controllers, guitar synths and so on all control sound modules. There are still keyboard controllers with sound modules on board, however, and it can be handy to have one at your disposal.

MIDI AND EFFECTS

All synths (controllers, sound modules, effects processors) communicate via a system known as MIDI, or Musical Instrument Digital Interface. MIDI is a system of interface cables that allows synths to talk to one another. For instance, let's say you have a keyboard controller and a sound module, and you want to play a sound. You connect a MIDI cable from your controller to your sound module. When you play a note on your controller, that action is translated into MIDI information that travels down the length of a MIDI cable and reaches another device (or sound module), which in turn triggers that same note. *Voila!* Instant sound. Your MIDI system can be as simple as this, or it can be extremely complex, with literally hundreds of synths all communicating simultaneously. Any synth or module should be able to send or receive MIDI information.

Effects processors are units designed to alter an existing sound. Reverbs, delays, echo devices, choruses, flangers and harmonizers are all effects processors. This is the final stage in your process of creating a sound, and the right-sounding reverb or chorus can make all the difference in a synth texture. A good reverb or delay effect can bring an otherwise dull synth sound to life. Effects processors are the recording engineer's tools, and a truly qualified synth whiz must be able to use them effectively as well.

SEQUENCERS AND COMPUTERS

A sequencer is a computer that inputs musical information (notes, volume changes, vibrato, pitch band, etc.), stores it in files and plays it back upon command. Anything that can be played on a synthesizer can be played back on a sequencer. It is basically a tape recorder without the tape. A computer is, for these applications, a powerful sequencer with printing and word processing capabilities.

For a composer, a sequencer is a powerful tool. With orchestra arrangements, you must write the parts on a score, send the score to the copyist, book a session—and finally, days later, you get to hear what you wrote. With a sequencer and several sound modules, an orchestrator with a little keyboard facility can get instant feedback by inputting the score parts into the sequencer, using appropriate sounds for each part. In a few minutes, you can be listening to a reasonable facsimile of your orchestration.

SETTING UP AT HOME

It is not necessary for you to own a synthesizer to be able to write for one, but it goes without saying that the more you know about a subject, the more informed your judgment will be. It's handy to have a keyboard around on which to try things out, and messing around with weird sounds in the privacy of your own room can be a lot of fun! It really is a blast to listen to sounds you have never heard before and then apply them to your music. It's like having an orchestra at your fingertips.

There are several types of synthesizers. The earliest synths were analog-based, and they are still around. Vintage synths like the Mini-Moog, the Prophet 5 and the Jupiter 8 will always have a place in a professional synth rack. They are big and bulky, with lots of knobs and sliders, and instantly programmable from the front panel. But times have definitely changed. Nowadays, your synths are apt to be controlled by computer, with a large library of preset sounds—and instead of a big, bulky thing with a lot of knobs to hang on to, there's one lone slider that accesses all the programming parameters internally. Because of this situation, many (if not most) synth players don't bother to program their synth sounds; they just use the factory presets that are shipped in the unit. I am not going to delve into programming in this chapter, but it is important to have a bit of background on the hardware you will be using.

In addition to analog synths (which tend to have a warm quality), there are digital synths (based on algorithms), LA (or linear additive synthesis) synths, workstations (the ideal composer's tools, with sounds, effects and sequencers all in one unit) and samplers (a sampler records a sound digitally and applies it tonally to a keyboard). Any good keyboardist who plays sessions for a living will probably have a wide selection of different synths, because each instrument has different sound qualities and strengths.

It is not necessary for you as a composer to have every single one of these types of synthesizers, unless that is of particular interest to you. What you *do* want is to have enough hardware to be able to create musically whatever you need.

This will vary from person to person. One person may be satisfied with a modest keyboard to check voicings on. Someone else may want the ability to play back complex orchestrations with a sequencer. Still another type of composer may want to do all his or her own synth programming and performing, which requires a very extensive studio setup.

One way to get started is to get a workstation. A workstation is a synth with everything built into it. It has a keyboard, it is multitimbral (it plays many sounds at once), it has an effects processor (or two or three) and it has a sequencer. The memory space available on a workstation is usually somewhat smaller in comparison to a computer-based synth setup, but it can meet your multipurpose needs, albeit in a somewhat more limited fashion. It has all the elements of more powerful setups in one economical package. For the composer on a budget, it is definitely the way to go.

If you want a more powerful setup to play back your compositions and orchestrations, you will need to spend more money. For this you will require:

1. a sequencer or computer;

2. a controller—a keyboard synth would be the logical choice; and

3. one or more sound modules—this is where you can go overboard.

The more voices you have to work with, the more flexibility you will have. But how many do you need? If you write complex arrangements, you may require several multitimbral sound modules. You'll probably want to get a sample player (a sound module that plays samples of orchestral instruments) to approximate your orchestral timbres. Another option is to get a sampler and create your own samples. It depends on how deeply you want to get into it.

My suggestion is to start simply. Go to your local music store and talk to the person in the keyboard department. Start with a relatively small setup. Later, after you have experimented a little, you can always add on to it.

COMPOSER VERSUS PLAYER

It is true that many composers do their own synthesis (in conjunction with a programmer, usually). If you have the time and the ability, you can certainly program your own synths. You must decide for yourself how deeply you want to delve into the world of electronic music. Keep in mind, though, that just as a violinist spends his or her whole life perfecting the sound of the violin, so the synth specialist dedicates himself or herself to creating new and interesting textures. It is nice to know that there are always specialists in the field who can be hired to produce the results you require in your music.

VOCABULARY

One of the most important things for a composer or conductor to be able to do is communicate ideas clearly to the musicians in the orchestra. In working with your synthesist, it is always helpful to know a bit about the language of synthesizers and electronics. Sometimes the hardest thing for a player to deal with is trying to figure out what sound the composer wants to hear. *THE MOST IMPORTANT INFORMATION TO GIVE YOUR SYNTH PLAYER IS THE KIND OF SOUND YOU WANT TO HEAR.* I would estimate that for most situations, 80 to 90 percent of your synthesist's time will be spent programming the sounds and sequenced patterns required for the piece. If you can steer him or her in the right direction, it will save you valuable studio time and money.

Example #1

Bells with Echo ($\quad$ = 104)

Low Male Voices with String Basses (slow attack)

In most cases you will know what you want to hear. But every so often an occasion arises on which you want to stretch yourself compositionally and work with new sounds and textures. In these instances it is very helpful to meet with your programmer ahead of time to discuss in detail what you are thinking about doing. If you have taped examples of similar sounds and effects, these can be invaluable aids in achieving what you need. You could describe what is in your mind from now until forever and not succeed in communicating effectively what could be made clear to your programmer in just a few seconds of listening to a recorded example.

Of course, it is very helpful to know a little bit about synthesis and to have at least a rudimentary vocabulary relating to synthesizers. But absolutely the most important aspect of using synthesized sounds in your orchestrations is to be clear in your own mind about what these sounds should be accomplishing in a musical sense. You should know, for instance, whether your sound should create a blending effect to enhance your orchestral textures or whether you need a color that will cut through and be featured like a solo. As with other solo sounds, it is good practice not to write too thickly, so that the solo sound can be heard well enough above the supporting instruments.

A word of warning: if you are going to build a piece around a particular synthesized sound, don't leave yourself open to surprises on the day of the session. Know ahead of time what to expect, so that if it doesn't work quite the way you had hoped, you can make the necessary adjustments. Also, in some cases, you may have written for a sound that will require a specific instrument or a special sequenced program that may not be readily available. You definitely don't want to find this out at 9:00 in the morning, a few minutes before your record date!

If you know what you want, and if your keyboardist gives you a sound that is close but not quite on the money, you should be able to help him or her fine-tune that sound so that it works for you. In most cases, it is a matter of adjusting the attack time or the release time of the sound. Maybe the color is a bit too bright or too dark for what you had in mind. In most cases, these are simple adjustments that an experienced programmer should be able to make in a few short moments.

The following is a very basic list of examples and definitions which should help you in communicating with your synth player or programmer. This is not intended to be a comprehensive list but merely a starting point in your introduction to synthesizer terminology.

ADSR: A sound has four basic elements: attack, decay, sustain and release. These elements can be referred to as the sound envelope. To change the envelope is to alter one of these four basic characteristics.

If the sound you hear seems to be speaking late, or sounds like it is behind the rest of the band, chances are that the attack time is too slow. A faster attack time means that when you play the sound from the keyboard, it will respond more quickly. With a maximum attack time (0 or 1 on most synths) you should get instantaneous response from your synth. A slower attack means that you may have to hold the key down a few moments while the sound fades in.

If you want to hear a sound sustain longer on each note, then it is possible that you need to adjust your *release time*. The release time is the amount of time that the sound is sustained after you release your finger from a key. A release time of one second means that after you pick your finger up from the key, the sound will continue for one second before it stops.

Chorusing is the slight detuning of a sound in order to make it sound thicker. Other types of effects similar to chorusing are *phase shifting, harmonizing, pitch shifting* and *flanging*. You can usually build these effects into a synth sound, but they can also be added later by using an external processing unit.

When you're working with a sound that is a bit thin, adding a chorus or a flanged effect can be extremely helpful, as it will thicken the texture.

Reverb is simply ambience (or reverberation), which can be added as an effect. Reverbs can sound like huge concert halls, small rooms or even your garage if that's what you want. This is the finishing touch for many synth sounds.

Delay (or *echo*) is different from reverb in that it is an effect based on the repetition of your sound. In other words, you combine your original sound with a delay that causes the sound to repeat however many times you want it to.

Dry means without reverb or processing. If you hear a sound that has too much reverb or delay, you might ask your programmer to "dry it up" a little.

Wet is the opposite of dry. Let's say you have a string sound that you want to make sound more distant, farther in the background. In this case, you would make the sound "wetter" by adding reverb or delay.

Pitch bend is a performance effect used to slide from note to note (like portamento), usually controlled by the use of a pitch wheel. Pitch bend is an invaluable tool. Many people do not know that the performance of a synth sound is sometimes equally as important as the timbre of that sound. For instance, you might take the sound of a steel guitar for granted, unless you play one yourself. But the performance includes a tremendous amount of various types of pitch bending between strings, the use of pedals and so on. If your synth player is sharp, he or she will know that an effective synth guitar sound requires not only a good timbre but also the adept use of pitch bending techniques.

Modulation is another performance effect usually controlled by a pitch wheel, or sometimes by *aftertouch*. (Aftertouch is the exertion of pressure while holding down a key.) This can be used as a type of vibrato.

Just as pitch bend is extremely effective in the performance of many sounds, so is the use of a *volume pedal*. In order to create crescendos and diminuendos for a string section timbre, or swells for a brass choir, a volume pedal is essential.

Sometimes, you might hear your synthesist using a sound that has too much attack or bite to it. In such an instance, you could suggest that he or she "pedal it in" in order to soften the attack. The same thing applies to an abrupt release: "pedal it out."

If you want a mechanical, computerized effect—that of a machine, with no human imperfections—use a *sequencer*. With a sequencer, you can have a computer perform the part for you perfectly; all you need to do is program it.

I have seen a number of composers who do some of their writing on their sequencers. Some of these writers bring their sequences into the session and give them to the synthesist, which eliminates the need for that player to spend time programming while on the date. Then the synthesist can spend the time practicing the part or programming the timbre. This is certainly not a necessary step, but it shows you just how far you can take programming if you want to.

BLENDING TEXTURES

Acoustic (orchestral) instruments tend to have a warm sound quality, in contrast to synths, which, relatively speaking, have a colder sound. Both qualities are valid musically, but you should know the role you want your electronics to play in the sound of your music ahead of time. If you want your music to sound very electronic, then you will probably go with primarily synthesized textures, with maybe a few acoustic instruments for solos and to warm up the overall sound. Or maybe you don't want to hear the synths much at all, but you need them for breadth and body, in which case you will write them to blend in with your acoustic instruments.

For a while, producers were using synthesizers to replace orchestral instruments as a cost-cutting measure. This is not done very much any more, mainly because everyone discovered that it ultimately wasn't any cheaper to use three synth players in lieu of fifteen string players, what with equipment rentals, cartage costs and double-scale rates being what they are—not to mention the fact that no matter how hard you try, a synthesizer playing a string pad will never sound like twenty violinists playing in unison. But if you combine your twenty string players with your synth pad (written in an idiomatic and complementary way), then you will have an incredibly gorgeous sound that combines the best of both the orchestral and electronic worlds.

Don't write synth parts to replace what should be performed by acoustic instruments! You have to play to the strengths of your instruments, and it is unrealistic to think that synths (which do certain things quite well) are able effectively to do everything that an orchestra can do. You can achieve some stunning synth orchestral effects through layering textures and so on, but you must write somewhat differently from the way you would for an orchestral configuration.

For instance, in an orchestral situation where you might give the violins a fast ostinato figure to create fire and motion, you probably would have to write the part differently for a synth. Writing the same figures for a synth string sound, even performed by a skilled player, you're liable to end up with a part that sounds more like a calliope than a string ostinato.

Example #2

Strings

String Synth. (Simplified)

In the preceding example you could have the strings play the fast run while the synth augments the sound with the simplified part.

You can use a sequencer to create something fast and flourishy that is different from the example above, yet thematically similar. You can be creative, because with a sequencer you can write absolutely anything and not be limited by an instrument's (or player's) technical facility. All you need to do is make sense musically.

Example #3

Bell Shimmer Sequence

When writing brasslike figures for synth keyboard, remember that you can't triple-tongue on a keyboard, and repeated tonguing figures are next to impossible to play. (The wrist simply can't spring back to the keyboard as quickly as a brass player can flutter-tongue.) Unless you have a sequencer to program what is not playable, it is better to fill out the part chordally and leave the fast stuff for your horns and brass.

Example # 4

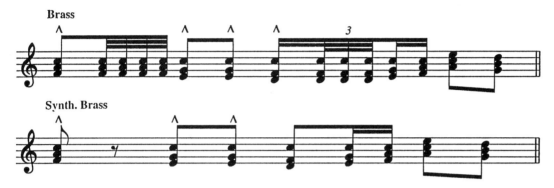

Again, your synth part should support the busier part that the brass is playing.

To achieve the classic synth effect of the filter envelope opening, you can specify what you need in a couple of ways: you can use crescendo and diminuendo markings, or you can describe the sound of the filter opening—or both.

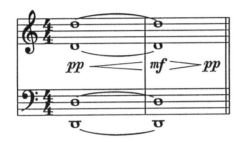

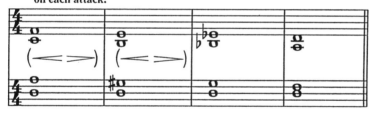

Open filter envelope on each attack.

When writing for a huge sound, like a big orchestral hit, be aware that the sound very often will be composed of several octaves and intervals. Such a sound will usually work best as a single note; if you write it as a chord, you will get some very thick harmonies, which you probably won't want.

(Correct) Orch. Hit

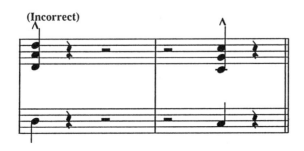

(Incorrect)

Using delay effects can be very effective, especially if the delay is locked in time with the music. Be sure to give the synth player the click rate or metronome marking at the top of the page.

BE NICE TO YOUR SYNTHESISTS

There are ways that you can make life easier for your electronic musicians—and they basically amount to making sure that you don't ask the impossible.

One of the hardest things for a synth player to deal with is the situation in which a composer writes four sounds in the course of five measures. Now, where there is a will there is a way, and somehow the parts always get played (although after such an experience, I, as a synthesist, have been known to run screaming into the studio parking lot). But as a composer, you should be aware that the more things you ask your synth player to do, the more things he or she will have to concentrate on and to deal with. Many times (though not always) your synthesist will need to sacrifice quality of sound in order to achieve what you asked for.

If you want a killer bass sound, for instance, your programmer may want to layer four or five synths together to produce that sound. Fine. But if you also wrote three other sounds in the course of that particular 20-measure cue, the programmer may not be able to use all those synths on one bass sound; he or she will have to divide them up on the other three sounds you wanted. Hey, if you need all those sounds, then you have to have them. But it is better not to stretch your synth players too thin. Don't make them switch sounds every couple of measures; needless to say, you will not endear yourself to them—and, more important, you will sacrifice a certain amount of sound quality in requiring them to diversify their musical tasks.

Another rule of thumb: whenever humanly possible, *try to write one sound at a time.* There are several reasons for this. When one synth sound comes out of a stereo mixer (combined with stereo reverb effects, etc.), you get a beautiful stereo imaging effect with a real depth of texture. *Whenever possible, always try to run your synthesizers in stereo.* If this doesn't seem that important, then try comparing a programmed stereo patch with its mono version. Just take your stereo sound and pan both channels up the middle. You will have a similar sound, but with a fraction of the depth. With luck, you will be able to afford two synthesists to produce these sounds simultaneously out of two separate stereo racks, or at least have the option of overdubbing the second sound later on in the day. But at the very least, you should know the consequences of writing a part with two sounds going at the same time.

With more than one sound at a time (say, a Rhodes sound in the left hand and a horn sound in the right hand) you create a balance problem for the mixing engineer. Don't misunderstand; this is a workable situation, simply not an optimal one. It's better to keep things uncomplicated. One way around this is to have your synthesist send the Rhodes out the left channel and the horn out the right channel. But then you sacrifice your stereo imaging.

As a conductor, you will have another set of circumstances to consider—that of programming time in an orchestral situation. In setting up for a musical cue or take, *your synth players (and your percussionists) will* ALWAYS *need more time than everyone else to get set up.* Remember that in virtually every case, a synth player is producing a different timbre on every cue, and so he or she must have a few moments (and in certain special situations, several minutes) to get ready. Conductors sometimes forget this fact, undoubtedly because everyone else in the orchestra is visibly ready to go. You look around from the podium and the strings and brass and woodwinds have all turned to the next piece of music, instrument in hand. Since the electronics contingent is almost always in the back of the band, it's easy to forget about them as they're quietly getting ready. So make a point of asking them if they're set before you give the downbeat; they will appreciate it more than you'll ever know.

Knowledge is power. The more you learn about the world of electronic music and synth colorations, the more you will be able to add to your orchestrational abilities. You will find yourself thinking in a completely new way about the nature of sound, and subsequently you will discover new and exciting ways to combine sounds, giving your compositions an added depth.

> *Another story about a no-talent composer-conductor in Hollywood goes like this:*
>
> *Wanting to impress the musicians with his superior knowledge of music, this particular individual was looking through his scores prior to an upcoming recording session.*
>
> *He noticed a section for the trombones marked "quasi horn," which he marked with red pencil. During rehearsal he arrived at that particular spot and stopped the orchestra.*
>
> *"Gentlemen! If you please, at measure 41, more quasi, if you don't mind—much more quasi."*

CROSS-SCORING

"*C*ross-Scoring" is a term that I made up when I first started to write instrumental music for publication. What it means is that when a work is orchestrated for either concert band or orchestra it will sound good with minimum instrumentation.

This technique is basically applied to school works of a simpler level, those that are geared toward grade school and junior-high ensembles. The technique can be applied, albeit to a lesser degree, to more mature, serious works (of greater difficulty). The drawbacks of using cross-scoring is that the end result sometimes becomes a little too "straight vanilla."

First and foremost in importance, is the cueing of solos. An oboe solo, for example, would be best cued for a solo clarinet or a flute, or even both. A French horn solo, depending on the range, could go to a baritone horn or a saxophone. Many of these choices might not be artistically correct, but they do enable the piece to be played when certain key players are missing. With an orchestra, the same philosophy applies. An English horn solo would be cued, and perhaps a bassoon solo.

The first step is to set up a basic instrumentation. There are certain instruments that *must* be there, otherwise there is no sense in even writing the composition. One must also recognize the fact that there is no perfect solution to cross-scoring. It is simply a way of getting an organization of limited means to sound as complete as possible.

The instrumentation that I use is as follows: (An extension of this would include one French horn, and a baritone horn.)

Band	Orchestra
one flute	one flute
three clarinets (I, II and III)	one oboe
two alto saxophones	two clarinets
one tenor saxophone	two trombones
three cornets (trumpets)	two trumpets
two trombones	two trombones
one tuba	one alto sax (optional)
two percussion	one tenor sax (optional)

	Orchestra (Continued)
—	two French horns
—	violin I
—	violin II
—	viola
—	cello
—	bass
—	two percussion

In orchesrating using cross-scoring, the most obvious preliminary step is to approach the piece using the limited instrumentation only. After this is completed, then go back and fill in the rest of the parts. It is a thankless task, but the end result will be something that is very practical.

I remember a lecture given in college by an expert on the music of the Baroque period, mainly liturgical. He said that quite often on Sunday mornings, the conductor never really knew who was going to show up and who wasn't. Therefore, the use of harmonic chord symbols in keyboard-continuum parts allowed missing parts to be filled in.

Again, let me emphasize that this technique is mainly intended for young organizations playing simple music. Although one can apply certain aspects of it to more advanced writing, the application has its limits. If you are writing a symphony, you assume that it will be played by a full orchestra or symphonic band.

TRICKS (OR THINGS THAT WORK)

*F*irst of all, I don't think that "tricks" is the proper word for what this chapter is all about. But "things that work" is definitely what it is all about! You will not find these suggestions in any theory or harmony books, and it is very doubtful that you ever learned them in school. You pick them up like most things—through trial and error, advice from musicians and quite often from listening and looking at other writers' scores. Many of these examples will address themselves to bands or orchestras of limited means. If you have a huge ensemble at your disposal, you have an embarrassment of riches and thus can do whatever you wish. Other examples will concern themselves with players of limited ability.

SIMPLIFICATION OF RAPID 16TH-NOTE PASSAGES

Nothing terrifies young players more than a lot of fast 16ths. The following passage offers a way out of the problem. Although I have clarinets I and II in the example, it could just as well be for flutes, trumpets or violins. The result will be practically the same as the original configuration.

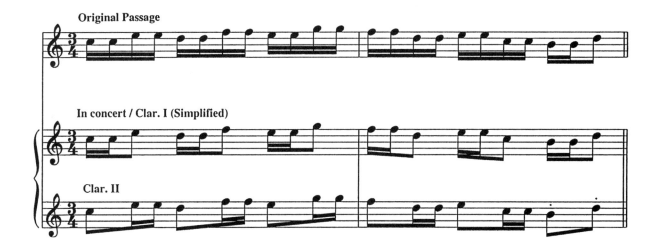

IF YOU WANT A HUGE, MASSIVE ACCENTED CHORD

This is meant for a band or orchestra of limited means, although its primary application is for writing film music. The piano, in this instance (along with the percussion), gives the accented note its harmony. By keeping the winds and strings on the unison, more power will be achieved (if strings are available, double stops would add to the power). The second example assumes that a few more instruments are available. You will note that the piano chord does not use the notes B or F.

In many instances when I wanted the effect of this chord to be dissonant, I would have the pianist use his left forearm on the lowest black keys, and his right forearm and palm on the lowest white keys. This makes a formidable percussive accent.

Example A   Example B

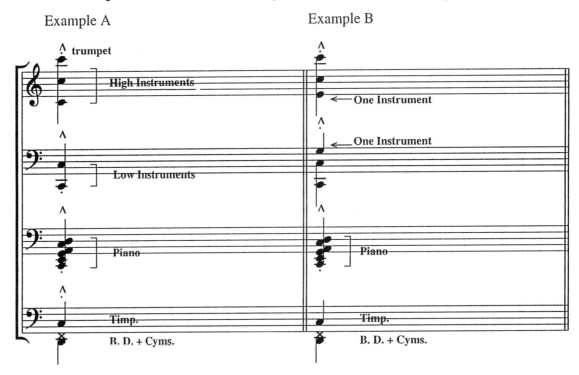

In many of my seminars, I address various aspects of string writing. This is the one area where no one has been able to improve on the great composers of the past. A small but important point concerns itself with unison writing. If one has a normal complement of strings, then the first example on the next page would, of course, be used. However, if you are short of players, the second example will work just fine. You will not miss the middle octave as much as you think. The overtones created by the top and bottom registers will give you a powerful sound. The third example is totally worthless. Two octaves sound thin and weak no matter how many players you have.

These examples, by the way, are meant for situations when strings have the melody.

The last example, with all the violins on a single note, would sound brilliant for a recording but would be rather weak in the concert hall. The one exception would be a very large complement of violins I and II.

For the voicings of the first two examples to work properly, the top violin line cannot go too low. If it does, the effect will be lost and the sound will be muddy.

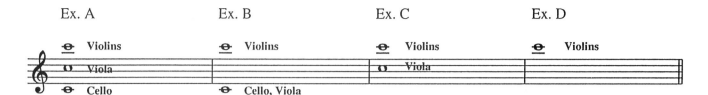

Ex. A   Ex. B   Ex. C   Ex. D

Violins   Violins   Violins   Violins
Viola   Viola
Cello   Cello, Viola

MAKING PROPER CHORAL ENTRANCES

Usually when a mixed chorus starts singing, a piano chord or pitch is sounded and everyone begins. Because perfect pitch is in short supply, more often than not, the beginning chord is just a little out of tune. A way out of this is to start on a unison. Granted, this may not be practical in all situations, but it's something to consider.

Let's assume a piece has started and after a bit there is a piano or instrumental interlude. At this second entrance there will not be the luxury of the pitch pipe. Better that everyone starts on a single note. It may be octaves, because of the difference in men's and women's ranges, but it will be more effective. Besides, who cares about the difference?

Again, I say, keep it simple. That philosophy will never fail you. Keep in mind that with musical instruments you place your fingers somewhere and the proper note comes out—most of the time, anyway. Singers, however, have to "think" the note before they can produce it. Make their life easier; your performance will be the better for it.

In your arranging, keep the skips to a minimum and avoid the tritone. If it's in the melody, that's something else, but skips and tritones are hard to sing in the inner voices. I have written many choral arrangements in which all the voices moved up or down one tone only. It can be done, it just takes a little thought. Again, these points are made for the benefit of those writing for less than top professional organizations. I have worked with choral groups who read extremely difficult material perfectly the first time and recorded it five minutes later. We do not always have the luxury of being able to work with these people.

From the beginning of time, I guess, musicians who perform for a living have always been asked to contribute their services gratis. Perhaps it is because there are so many amateurs among us. There is a great story about this kind of thing happening to the famous violinist Jascha Heifitz.

It just so happened that he was invited to a rather large soirée by a society matron. It was to be held in her New York Fifth Avenue mansion. During the phone conversation she asked Mr. Heifitz if he would mind bringing his violin and perhaps playing a few selections for the guests. Heifitz responded by saying he would, but in that case, he felt obligated to charge his usual fee of five thousand dollars. The society matron coldly responded, "Fine, but then I must ask you to not mingle and speak to the guests." Whereupon Heifitz replied, "If I do not have to speak to the guests, Madame, my fee will then be two thousand dollars."

CREATING TURBULENCE

A common technique in "creating turbulence" is the mixing of rhythmic patterns. This use of syncopation is probably the most common:

We can then add a trill, which will make it even more turbulent.

Another possibility is to mix up the rhythmic pattern, such as is found in the example below, from Mussorgsky's *Boris Godunov*. The violins and violas play 16ths in three octaves (very powerful), and the cellos and basses play 8th-note triplets in two octaves. The danger would occur if the low strings played the following figure, which would ruin everything:

THE USE OF THE MAJOR SECOND IN HARMONIC SITUATIONS

The use of this device has the advantage of introducing a neutral tonality to whatever you are writing. It also adds a very "airy" and pleasantly dissonant aura to your harmony. To achieve this effect, the third is usually left out, but it can be included. When the third is included, however, the neutral effect of the harmony disappears. For example, if you use the chord F–G–C it can work as either an F-major chord, a C seventh with suspended fourth or a plain C chord with a suspended fourth.

In the following example from John Williams's *E.T.*, the composer uses this chord with the added third. By the way, this kind of B-flat chord is probably the simplest form of what is commonly referred to as a "cluster" chord.

Selections from E. T.
(The Extra - Terrestrial)

CONDUCTOR

by John Williams
Scored for Band by
John Cacavas

UB161

Another example that utilizes this harmony is shown below. The chord is in the French horns and appears in measures 25, 27 and 29. The normal way to have harmonized this is simply to use an F-major chord. I wanted something a little more "biting" and nontonal, however. By substituting the G in the chord for the A, I accomplished my mission.

Overture Theatrique

John Cacavas

This type of harmony also works fine for strings, as shown below. It suggests a great "outdoorsy," majestic sound. The first example shows the effect without the third; the second one employs the third. The third example adds a D to the chord, which makes it fuller-sounding and more majestic. (The latter voicing, as shown, would be recommended for a string tremolo passage.) The unique thing about the first example is that your melody could contain any note of the F scale and it would sound fine. Introducing a B-flat in the second and third examples would create an awkward sound unless it were just a passing tone.

This chord also works very well for low percussive passages. The next example could be scored for low brass or strings:

Substituting the major second for the third opens up a lot of harmonic possibilities. Many chords that would ordinarily not work against a harmonic ostinato passage will work very well, as the following example shows:

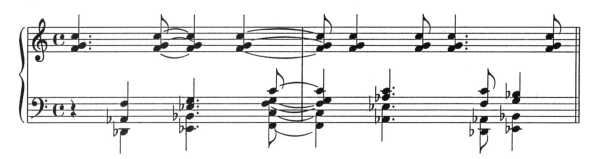

In the first bar (the F chord at the end of the measure in the bass clef), I omitted the third, although in this situation it would be fine. Also, this harmonic passage is somewhat dissonant, but it will not sound so to the ear. One of the tricks of an ostinato or repeated passage is that once the ear "tunes in" to the repetitiveness, most anything will work against it.

If I were to orchestrate the previous passage and wanted a full-blown effect, the treble clef would contain trumpets with violins, and woodwinds an octave higher. A piano playing both octaves would add a nice color. The bass clef would most likely contain the low brass.

Ira Gershwin recalled the time when he and Jerome Kern were
signed by MGM to write the songs for an MGM musical titled
Cover Girl. *It was a starring vehicle for Rita Hayworth and Gene*

Kelly. Kern came up with a particularly beautiful melody, which everybody at the studio fell in love with. However, Roger Edens, a music director at MGM who was assigned as associate producer of Cover Girl, *did not care for the lyrics that Ira had written. The song was called "Midnight Magic." He said that it was "not commercial enough."*

Fuming, Ira returned home and decided to write a lyric that would incorporate, as a joke, every commercial cliché he had ever heard of. He then hoped that he would be permitted to use his original lyric. When he and Kern went back to the studio to play it, much to Ira's chagrin, the producers thought the new lyric was terrific and was sure it would be a smash hit. And they were right.

The new lyrics started off like this:
"Long ago and far away,
I dreamed a dream one day."

At the end of his story, Ira went to his file and pulled out the yellow sheets of "Midnight Magic" and read them to me. They were good, but not as good as "Long Ago and Far Away."

When the movie came out, "Long Ago and Far Away" became an instant hit. It also sold more sheet music than any other song Ira had written up to that time. So much for clichés.

DO'S AND DON'TS

When a person first becomes a writer of music, everything is a "do," because experience has not yet demonstrated what will or will not work. What makes it frustrating is that sometimes something will work, and at other times it won't.

For example: harp, piano and bells in unison performed live in a slow tempo will be hard to perform accurately, even if the notation is simple. However, if you are writing film music and have a click track going for you, it will not be a problem.

In other words, something might work for one medium of performance but not for another.

We are all after the same thing. We want our music to sound good with a minimum of hassle. Better that rehearsal time be spent on the total effect than concerning itself with impossible ranges, bad fingerings and obvious problems of balance. Another thing to remember is that whatever piece you write, you should not have to be present to make it sound right. If you have to explain things at a rehearsal, you are not a professional composer or arranger.

This is especially true in writing for publication. Granted, you might have some performance notes included, which might address the subjective nature of the work, but just bear in mind that Bach, Beethoven and Mozart didn't need them, so why should you? In other words, let the music speak for itself. Program notes are another matter, since they deal with the intrinsic matter of the music and do not apply to performance. In my own works I try to keep performance notes to a minimum. My basic concern is in the areas of tempo. I always find that my published works (especially marches) are always played faster than indicated. I can never understand it. So let's move on to some thoughts about how to make our music sound better.

HOW TO MAKE YOUR MUSIC SOUND BETTER

DON'T HAVE A THIRD IN THE CHORD WHEN THE THIRD IS IN THE BASS

The chord will sound weak and terrible, whether it be major or minor. Here is an example:

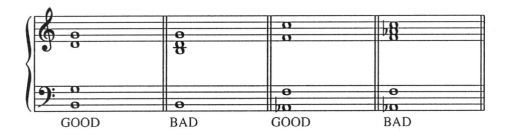

GOOD   BAD   GOOD   BAD

Now and then I am surprised to find that this rule has been broken in works (mainly for piano) of the old masters. However, in their defense, I should mention that it was usually when the third was in the melody. Besides, who am I to tell Haydn how to harmonize his piano solos?

DON'T DOUBLE THE THIRD UNNECESSARILY

If you have a whole symphony orchestra playing a major chord, just one audible instrument playing the third will be enough. One of the greatest recorded C-Major chords in history is the one John Williams employed in his main title sequence of *Close Encounters of the Third Kind*. In the opening sequence there is a high, dissonant string chord that just hovers there for almost a minute. Then there is a huge chord played by all the brass, winds and tuned percussion, which blows you out of your seat. Everyone is playing C's and G's, except the third trumpet, which has an E. I know this to be true because I wrote the symphonic band arrangement from his orchestral score. The chord, by the way, was a quarter-note with a heavy accent. So remember, don't double the third unnecessarily.

Here is the famous John Williams chord:

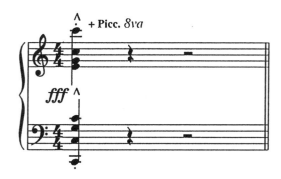

DON'T WRITE THINGS THAT WILL NEVER BE HEARD

I was studying the score of Mussorgsky's "Coronation Scene" from the opera *Boris Godunov* and found an amazing thing. There were several loud passages played by the entire orchestra and chorus, heavy and percussive. Meanwhile, only the bassoons were sustaining a low A and D in a series of tied-together dotted half-notes. There was no way they would be heard through this double-fortissimo din, even if there were a dozen of them. If Modest Mussorgsky had written this himself, I could understand. (After all, he was not known or regarded as an orchestrator.) However, this particular work was orchestrated by none other than Rimsky-Korsakov, whom we all know as a master of the craft. Why didn't he have them double the low strings, which was quite common at the time? Were the bassoonists friends of his who didn't play well? (This passage appears on p. 100 of the original Russian edition.) To add insult to injury, on p. 106, the two bassoons are the sole purveyors of a low G trill—again, against the entire orchestra and chorus. Moreover, it lasts for 15 measures without a breath.

I can just see those two bassoonists at rehearsal, jumping up, shaking their fists and beseeching the ensemble, "Lighten up, for God's sake." After all, bassoons can only blow so loud.

If I ever get to heaven, I'm going to look up good old Nicolai Rimsky-Korsakov and ask why he did it. I'll bet Mussorgsky was a little mad, too.

DON'T WRITE THINGS SO HARD THAT THEY CAN'T BE PLAYED PROPERLY

Keep it simple. How many times have you heard that? Well, it's true. When you're composing, you fool yourself sometimes. You go over something so many times that it is all perfectly clear, not realizing that the audience hears it only once. Therefore, it must be clear and uncluttered. That's why most arrangers are not good songwriters. They know too much and become confused by side issues when they should only be concerned about melody. Some of the greatest songwriters in history couldn't even read music. It makes one think, doesn't it?

The thing I, as a film composer, have heard most often from the producers and directors that hire me is to "thin it out"—drop instruments, and so forth. In other words, anything to make it more direct and to the point. Fancy orchestration can become your enemy, obscuring the main thrust of what you composed. Too much cleverness can get you fired.

None of this is meant to imply that difficult music is not good. What I am trying to get across is that if it is difficult for no good reason, *then* it is wrong. If you can make your statement *easier*, then do it. You will impress no one by writing needlessly difficult music.

I was talking to a cellist one time regarding an upcoming concert she was preparing. She mentioned that they were doing Wagner and had only two rehearsals. I remarked that only two rehearsals for Wagner seemed unrealistic, and she agreed.

"We only hit the highlights," she said. "Sometimes on the most difficult passages, we just play the most important notes."

Agreed, Richard Wagner was a genius and wrote some of the world's greatest music. Perhaps in his day, there were unlimited rehearsals with the same orchestra, which resulted in a kind of consistent perfection in performance. However, in real life this isn't always the case.

DON'T WRITE BAD FINGERINGS OR DIFFICULT-TO-PLAY NOTES

It's not a hard thing to walk up to a trumpet player and ask him or her what the most difficult notes are to play in tune. For example, the low C-sharp is not easy to play properly. If possible, avoid it. Go to a trombone player and ask him, "Is it hard going from low B-flat to B-natural?" If so, be careful in using it. As an ex-saxophone player, I know that low B-natural to C-sharp in a fast passage is next to impossible, so why write it? All you are doing is setting yourself up for a bad performance. In the back of my mind is the low D on an English horn. Even with the top professional players in Hollywood, it is a note that might end up with a squawk, or at best, an unusually hard attack. Changing pedals on the harp . . . fingerings on the violin . . . timpani tunings—all these things can be avoided if you talk to a player and take notes on prospective problems with the mechanics of the instrument.

If an instrumentalist is faced with several of these problems on his part, psychologically his or her performance has to suffer. The performer will be focusing on the problems, and this can't possibly be good. In the haste of writing a film score, I have sometimes forgotten some of these no-nos. I've quite often announced to the orchestra that if there are some notes that present problems, let me know and I'll provide alternatives. It doesn't happen that often, but when it does, this saves a lot of unnecessary trouble.

One of my pet peeves is a pizzicato string bass note that ends up with a "thud" instead of ringing out. Not being an expert on the instrument, I would add a notation to the part to play it up or down an octave in order to eliminate the offending sound. This never failed to eliminate the thud.

Be careful of ranges: certain instruments, such as flutes, are inaudible in their extreme low register unless they are amplified. An oboe written too low is audible, but not particularly effective or useful. Give it to the English horn or bassoon. DO NOT WRITE MUSIC THAT MIGHT EMBARRASS THE PLAYER, NO MATTER HOW PROFICIENT HE OR SHE IS!

WHEN USING MULTIREGISTERED BLOCK HARMONY, KEEP IT CONSISTENT

For the sake of illustration, let us use three-part harmony in this example. I don't know why, but if we use the block technique and add another note in just one of the blocks, it seems to lack clarity in performance. If it is a C-seventh chord and we're using C, B-flat and E, the addition of the G in only one block doesn't work as well. Obviously it won't be a disaster if we add the note, but it's better to keep it consistent. Here is the example in its proper form, followed by the improper form:

Note that in the second example, the middle blocking has the extra note. Now, if this were to be a four-way block, then there would be no problem. All four voices would be used. However, if we introduced a fifth harmony note, then the original premise would hold. Keep everything consistent. This philosophy really only applies to exposed, melodic situations. If these chords were accented, short notes, then it wouldn't make much difference. If this melody were conceived using only thirds, then again the addition of another harmony note would not be appropriate.

> *David Raksin is certainly one of Hollywood's most celebrated composers of motion-picture scores.* Laura, The Bad and the Beautiful, Forever Amber *and* The Secret Life of Walter Mitty *are just a few of his contributions to the screen.*
>
> *One night we were having a composer's guild meeting in our home, and on his way out he told me this story: he was approached by a producer who wanted him to score a film that was just about to commence shooting. The conversation went something like this:*
>
> *Producer: "I would like a score just like* Laura.*"*
>
> *David: "Fine, I'd be happy to. Just film another* Laura.*"*

PROOFREAD YOUR MUSIC

The thing that really differentiates a professional from an amateur is the number of mistakes in the music, especially in the individual parts. Nothing is more discouraging in rehearsal than finding measures left out, wrong key signatures and just plain wrong notes. Professionals make mistakes; to state otherwise would be ludicrous. However, professionals carefully go over what they have written, for in their case time is money.

Proofing your music is all the more important if you copy your own parts. Although mistakes in the score are not heard, the instrumental parts are where they turn up.

I remember one time at a recording session in New York, the well-known film conductor Jack Shaindlin was recording Morton Gould's score to *Windjammer* for the soundtrack album. I had been working for Gould as an orchestrator at that time, so I went along with Morton to the studio. This was in the early 1960s, when stereo was in its infancy, and the sound coming from the orchestra was glorious. During a break in the recording, a woodwind player raised his hand and shouted "Hey, Jack, I gotta wrong note in bar 46."

"Well, play the right one, for God's sake!" shouted Shaindlin in response.

Naturally everyone on the stage hooted, and the hapless woodwind player figured it out.

Top professional players can often correct a mistake without even asking the conductor or composer. They just know. With less skilled players, it is just the opposite. Sometimes they'll play wrong notes consistently and not even know they're doing so. The ability to discern subtle mistakes comes with performing maturity.

After I finish a score page, I usually go over it while it is still fresh in my mind. Outside of accents, fermatas and so on, I'll save the dynamics for later. I write all my scores in transposed pitch, and I find that area is usually the one that has the errors. I never use key signatures in my film music (unless it is an arrangement of a song), so I don't have to worry about accidentals as much. I also cancel accidentals in the following bar just to play it safe.

In film music, I number every bar and the copyist also does so on the parts. This makes it much easier in rehearsal to go straight to a problem if you know, for example, that it's exactly in measure 16. This practice, however, is not practical for published music. I usually mark every eight measures or so.

The biggest nightmare is finding, when you first run something through, that measures are missing. This takes an interminably long time to correct and is discouraging to all involved. A good copyist counts measures once he or she has finished a part. And a good composer or arranger will proof the full score.

I usually wait until I have finished a piece before I add the dynamics. This way I can see the work in its entirety and at the same time have a fresh look at it.

Now and then, of course, I'm tempted to throw it away and say to hell with it.

MAKE YOUR WRITING CLEAR, CONCISE AND LEGIBLE

When I was the director of publications for Chappell, a lot of manuscripts passed over my desk. I was always amazed to see so many songs that were squeezed into a few lines when the composer had a whole page he or she could have filled up. I also saw this in choral works and band pieces, where four bars to a score page would have been easier on the eye. Instead, eight or nine bars would be crowded onto the page.

Paper is not that expensive, and it behooves the creator to make the music easy on the eye. If a pen is not used, then the pencil should be dark enough to read easily. If a light pencil is used, then photocopy it. The reproduction will be darker.

Learn how to make proper noteheads, clefs and accidentals. Invest in a copying book (there are several on the market), and practice your craft. Nothing turned me off more quickly than getting a manuscript that looked like it had been written by a third-grader.

Double-check as you're writing, to be sure of the notes. If it's on the line, that's where it belongs—not somewhere in between. Make sure the stems are on the proper side of the notehead. It's all very simple, but you'd be surprised at how terrible a lot of manuscripts look. A note of explanation: the notes need not look like the work of a gifted copyist, but they must be accurate and readable. All one has to do is to look at the manuscripts of Bach, Beethoven and Mozart to realize their penmanship would never win any prizes. However, you know where the notes and accidentals are, and that's what counts. Those poor guys wrote with feathers and quills, too. Gotta give them credit.

Last but not least, do not use the cheap, thin manuscript paper. It's okay for sketching or making notes, but avoid it like the plague for your final work. Buy proper manuscript and score paper, and lots of it. You can usually get a discount on larger quantities.

DON'T USE COMPLEX METER CHANGES TO SHOW OFF

Obviously meter changes, and sometimes difficult ones, are the subjective wish of the composer to create a rhythmic pattern that he or she feels is necessary for the effectiveness of the work. However, in a piece written in 2/4 time, a bar of 6/16 coming out of nowhere just does not make sense. The effect can just as easily be brought about with accents, or by changing the time signature to 3/4. If it cannot be simplified, then the meter changes may become necessary—but use common sense.

I keep coming back to the same thing: make it as clear as you can. For every difficult compositional problem, there is usually a simpler solution.

When writing in units of four, that is, going from 2/4 to 4/4, then 3/4, and so on, there is no problem, because the execution of these meter changes does not present any great difficulty. Just make sure your reason for doing it makes sense musically. What meter changes do is alter the flow that has been established. In film music, it is done constantly to correspond to the action you are accompanying.

For young players, the arbitrary use of difficult meter changes can be devastating—with the exception of teaching pieces written just for that reason. In closing, I will say this: if you don't have to do it, then don't.

WRITING MUSIC FOR MOTION PICTURES AND TELEVISION

*T*he easiest part about scoring for films is that all you have to do is accompany something that's already done. It's not like having something played in a concert hall, where everyone pays attention to just the music. You can also hide behind sound effects (which often obliterates your music) and dialogue. You also receive a lot of hints about what to do. You know very well you're not going to play "Tiptoe through the Tulips" while some guy carrying an ax is chasing a woman!

The hard part is writing something *good*. The second-hardest part is to please the people who hired you, because if you don't, they will most certainly fire you—or, as they say in Hollywood, "you'll get your score dumped."

Generally speaking, motion pictures are a director's medium (in television, they're the producer's medium). In other words, you'll most likely be hired by a director for a movie and a producer for a television show. In either case, the thing to remember is that you've got to find out (if possible) what your employer wants to hear, musically speaking. I cannot stress this enough. Communication is the key to fashioning a score that will work, in addition to serving the wishes of the person hiring you. If you disagree with the musical ideas presented to you, then you must say so and try to reach a compromise. If a certain scene eludes you, then talk to your producer (or director). After all, this person has been living with the picture for months, while you've just been called in on it. It has been my experience that these people are always willing to give you leeway, and they're enthusiastic about music. As a matter of fact, several producers have mentioned to me that the scoring stage is one of the last vestiges of "show business." There's nothing like a live orchestra making music.

Aside from the various limitations you have to face, writing music for films is no different from writing any other kind of music . For example, if a very tender scene appears, you play it. But what happens ten seconds later when the scene changes to a barn dance in progress? You must make your statement in that ten-second period. In motion pictures, you get a chance to "stretch out" more than in television. TV tends to use more fast cuts, and music helps to define the action. In other words, you must learn to get in and out gracefully without being heavy-handed.

Another thing to remember is to go with the flow. If the picture is lazy, music should also reflect that feeling. There are certain kinds of sequences where one can "play against the picture." For example, if a car chase is taking place, one does not necessarily have to write a lot of fast music. You can play something atmospheric and ominous that might work just as well. You might consider the sound effects as part of your score—there will be plenty; you can count on that. When I was scoring *Airport '77*, there was a close-up of a 747's engines. Well, I never knew an airplane engine could be so loud! In other words, you must take into consideration which effects will be playing along with you. Don't fight the sound-effects editors; they usually win. So, go along with it and make it work for you. Once when faced with a scene of crashing oil derricks, fire sirens, screaming, shouting, explosions and everything else, I just had the basses, cellos and synthesizers hold their lowest C for the four minutes during the scene. The word "genius" was bandied about, as I remember. There's always a way out of situations like that, and they're usually simple.

Which brings me to another very important philosophy in film music: keep it simple. When the mind is trying to assimilate vision, dialogue, sound effects and music, you don't want to complicate things any more than they already are.

I am constantly amazed at what comes out of the speakers once the picture is dubbed. When you hear the playbacks in the studio, it is all quite wonderful—the stereo tracks booming out at you through those expensive speakers, the brilliance of the sound, all of it. But just wait until you hear your film when it comes out of a TV speaker, stereo or not. You'll wonder where all those musicians went. Did they just disappear? It is at that moment that you realize what you wrote was merely an *accompaniment* to everything else. There is also something quite mysterious that nobody talks about, called "atmosphere." Atmosphere is the kind of white sound that hovers in the background and competes with the sound effects to diminish your score. My only advice is not to fight it, because it is more powerful than you are. So, enjoy the thrill of seeing your name on the screen, spend the money and just hope you get hired again. If you've got a huge ego, don't expect the film business to feed it. Write operas, symphonies or ballets instead—those are the places for egos.

Nevertheless, it is an exciting business, and if you're lucky, your score may get a sound-track release, which will restore your music to all its glory.

I'm sure that if Mozart, Beethoven and Brahms were around today, they would probably take a crack at the movies and then complain when their scores got lost in the muddle. The trouble is that we are never satisfied. We enjoy the pursuit of excellence. So go after it.

SYNCHRONIZATION

There are basically four ways to match your music to film, some more accurate than others. These are stopwatch, click track, streamers and punches, and computer-driven programs. Unless certain "hits" are necessary and the internal timing is of no great importance, a stopwatch can be used. However, it is difficult to conduct while keeping your eye glued to a watch. Most scoring stages have very large clocks (over a foot in diameter), which are placed near the podium. This makes things a great deal easier. This technique can be used whether you are recording to picture or not.

An extremely accurate way of making sure of your timings is the click track. This is nothing more than an electronic metronome fed through earphones. It used to be that one had to figure out the increments mathematically. Several years ago, an enterprising music editor by the name of Carroll Knudsen figured out all the various tempos and corresponding clicks and put them into a book. This book, called *Project Tempo*, gives you all the information you need to score a film with exact timings in every case.

There are many books on the market that discuss the details of timing thoroughly, so I do not propose to go into them here. Any large music store will know about them.

The click track will enable you to make a hit, accent or change at any point, on any beat (or fraction thereof) during your musical cue. It is easy to figure out and foolproof. The machines that generate these clicks are more accurate than an electric metronome, and most studios are equipped with them. Before the advent of the digital click machines, holes were punched into the film, which sent an electronic pulse through the earphones.

If you have a music editor, he or she will give you warning clicks before the start of the cue, which will ensure a proper entrance. With a click track, it is easy to score an entire picture "wild," or without projection. In this case, the click machine will be started (at your desired click), and you can start anytime. The problems with recording "wild" is that you will be locked into the tempo from start to finish. However, it is possible to turn the clicks off—say, at the ending, if you want to slow down and finish off with the clock.

The click track is practically indispensable if you have a long, fast and exacting cue that requires a lot of "hits." The fact that every player has a headset will make accuracy a sure thing. Beware of being the only one with a headset. It will be very difficult to keep everyone together during a fast piece of music.

Regarding music editors, if you are lucky enough to get one your job will be much easier. Not only will he or she give you your timings and mark up your picture with streamers and punches but the editor will assist and guide you in such special features as overlays, wild hits and the like. Music editors are geniuses at repairing damage, adjusting your cue in case the picture gets changed after scoring and such magical things as that. If you are an inexperienced film composer and have the chance to work with an experienced music editor, just remember that he or she will know more than you do about the craft. I recall the early days of scoring "Kojak," when the studios were permitted to "track" (i.e., use existing prerecorded music from the series) a certain number of shows. I was always amazed at what the music editors chose to create a score. In many cases it was superior to what I would have written.

The next technique we will examine is using streamers and punches, which creates the "free timing" approach to conducting. A "streamer" is a diagonal line inscribed on the film that, when viewed through a projector, becomes a straight line moving vertically across the screen. When it reaches the end of the screen, a "punch" usually occurs, which pinpoints the timing. Your score would contain the timings, and a four-bar passage would look something like this:

In other words, this is the equivalent of a *visual* click track. With an M.M. marking of 60 to the quarter-note, we have four beats to a measure of 4/4. For free timing, the downbeat is always :00. If you wish to make an accelerando, then you have to adjust your timings, streamers and punches. This style of timing becomes your road map and is very effective when the character of your score is of a free or slow nature. That does not mean that you cannot effect hits or accent points. The streamer will lead you in, and the punch will be the impact point.

It is also possible to start a cue in free timing and then go into a predetermined click track. It is especially effective in a lyrical section that leads into a car chase or something similar. An example follows:

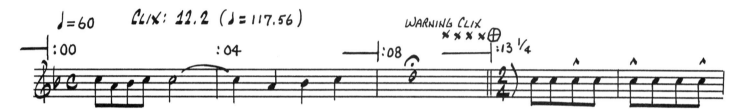

We start with free timing at four beats to the measure and reach a fermata at the third measure. After a few moments, we will hear four warning clicks in our new tempo, which begins at measure 4. If you have a click track book handy, you will find that the timing, :13.25, corresponds to beat 27 using a 12.2 click (M.M. ♩ = 117.56). The fifth click, which will come after the four warning clicks, will fall on the downbeat of measure 4. This is obviously a very simple solution to a situation, but basically the technique is the same and allows us to go from free timing to clicks in a manner that is foolproof.

When you use the click track book, the first thing you must ascertain is the tempo in which you are going to write your cue. Next, find the corresponding click. Check your cue sheets for important things that you want either to hit, to accent or to change the mood of. If they don't fall normally, then go either forward or backward a few pages to find the numbers that will fall more naturally. The click does not necessarily have to fall on a downbeat; accents between the clicks can be very effective.

Regarding the computer-driven programs, there are several systems that interface with various computers. They primarily work on the video system that uses the SMPTE timing rather than motion-picture film frames. These programs have the advantage of being extremely accurate, and it is also possible to make changes very quickly. They are capable of building variable click tracks as well. This type of timing system works especially well with self-contained electronic scores and is becoming more and more popular. It is obvious that as time goes by, these systems will become even more sophisticated, making the film composer's job a lot easier.

Today most music editors use these programs, and it has made their lives a lot simpler.

Say, for example, that you are writing a three-minute chase cue, and all of a sudden at the scoring session you find out that a few frames have been clipped out. Naturally this will knock your timings off. The computer will tell you exactly how to make your adjustments, by either adjusting the click track to make it fit or realigning the streamers or punches.

You will be able to find these programs wherever you buy your software products.

Much of the technology you will use depends on what kind of budget you have and what's available. If there is no money for a music editor, you will be doing a lot of the work yourself. If the film does not require exact timings, then your work will be easier. However, if you are faced with hitting fifteen different situations within a three-minute cue, you will have great problems without these mechanical aids.

In the last analysis, it is the music you write that counts. The synch devices only help to make sure everything fits.

SOURCE MUSIC

This is the term in film parlance that defines music that comes from a certain source (such as a radio, a singer in a nightclub, or a marching band at a football game). In other words, it comes from a "source" instead of being underscore.

Sometimes a producer will take artistic license and, having established a piece of source music, will keep it going even after the scene has shifted. From a realistic point of view it doesn't make sense, but artistically it may be a different matter.

Directors and producers often obtain the rights to hit tunes and incorporate them into their pictures. You'll see this most often in comedies and movies oriented toward the younger market.

Many motion pictures are scored entirely with records. In this case, the source becomes the underscore. *The Big Chill* comes to mind, as does Stanley Kubrick's *2001*. It is also a fact that many films do not need a score. The use of underscore just won't work. In this case, again, you will see recordings assuming the function of the music in the picture.

Licensing songs for a film can be expensive, so a composer is usually required to write the source music, especially for television. If a scene calls for a piano background in a piano bar, it really doesn't make a lot of difference what is playing, as long as it fits the mood. I've met many producers who always insisted on original pieces for source music under dialogue so the audience would not be distracted from the dialogue.

Source music can be very important in creating an immediate atmosphere. If the camera shows a shot of a café and twangy country music is leaking through, you know you're not at a posh club on New York's East Side. If, for example, your picture is set in the 1920s and a dance orchestra is playing at a country club, you'd better not arrange it like Stan Kenton. Source music, unlike underscore, can immediately project the listener into any era via the style of music and orchestration.

I remember doing one show that had a scene with a guy flipping a car radio tuner constantly. The sequence lasted only about fifteen seconds, but in addition to a couple of announcers, I had to create two different rock-and-roll bands; a piece of Vivaldi, a Frank Sinatra sound-alike and a dance orchestra. Each piece only lasted a couple of seconds, but it had to be done that way.

Unless it's a live performance integral to the film, most source music is recorded separately on the scoring stage. When you see a piano player in a bar, he's just pretending to play. He might play a few notes before the dialogue starts, but after that it's strictly visual. Otherwise the playing would be on the dialogue track, which is a big no-no.

In many instances, underscoring comes in over some existing source music. In that case, the score is called an overlay. To work properly, the score should be in a different tonality from the source. It usually happens at the end of a scene, and often on the dubbing stage the mixer does a cross-fade on the two pieces. Overlays can be dramatically effective. A good example would be, say, two men having a conversation at an ice-skating rink. The source music might be the "Skater's Waltz," coming from a loudspeaker. One of the men might make a threat to the other, at which time a very ominous low bass and cello line might intrude. The men have not left the locale, so the "Skater's Waltz" is still blaring away. The introduction of the low overlay helps to underscore the ominous turn the scene has taken. Take care not to make an overlay too complicated. To work effectively, it should be in a different tessitura from the source and, in this particular case, it must be very slow moving. If it gets too busy it will not work, and chances are that it will be discarded on the dubbing stage. If the source music was a solo violin, for example, then the overlay could be more ambitious. It's contrast we're after.

For the most part, you will be confined to whatever instrumentation you have for your film in order to create the source. God help you if you are doing a low-budget television show, and all of a sudden six bagpipers appear on the screen. If you have a synthesizer sample, however, you could be saved. Obviously there will be times when the producer is forced to license some kind of outside music, especially if he wants something to accompany the Ballet Russe!

Often you won't have to write endings for your source material, since the music often fades out while in progress. Make sure that this is discussed and agreed upon; otherwise you might find yourself being cursed when the producer decides to start the music earlier. Again, communication with the boss is the key.

Make sure that your source music does not interfere with the dialogue. An intimate tête-à-tête for two lovers won't be served well by a trio of blaring trumpets. If the scene is in a nightclub and the music is not visual, you use a solo guitar or piano. If it's established that the room might have piped-in music, then you could opt for a larger group. I remember in the motion picture *Once upon a Time in America* there was a sequence of source music with a group consisting of a clarinet, drums and banjo playing "Amapola." The film was set in the 1930s, and it was just perfect.

We are surrounded by "source" music in everyday life. Walking down the street, we hear transistor radios, Muzak in elevators and street musicians earning a few bucks. It is a very integral part of the total musical scenario of the picture we are scoring.

The next example is a typical cue sheet as prepared by a music editor. The beginning describes the action that has transpired in order to remind the composer rather than force him or her to view the whole film again. Each film editor has his or her own style of describing the action on film. Following are what the abbreviations on the enclosed cue sheets mean:

CAM.	= Camera
CU	= Close-Up
DAY	= Daytime
EST. EXT. L.S.	= Establishing Exterior Long Shot
EXT.	= Exterior
FG	= Foreground
F.S.	= Full Shot
INT.	= Interior
M.C.U.	= Medium Close-Up
L.S.	= Long Shot
MED. SHOT	= Medium Shot
OS	= Offstage
VO	= Voice-Over

A good music editor gives you any action and dialogue that follows your cue. Again, the more information you have, the better. In the following cue from "Columbo," I decided to do the sequence in free timing, since it was to be slow and moody. There are several streamers and punches to guide me along my 34-second journey, with only a couple of synch points to worry about. The hits that I employed were very subtle, just enough to acknowledge the change of view. At 30:03, I struck my final chord, which coincided with a voice-over dialogue bit that then faded out for an ending. The actual tailout would occur a few seconds after 34:73.

The nature of the music was ominous and slow in tempo.

Production: Columbo **Production #:** 64110 **Episode:** Grand Deceptions
Cue: 3m1
Begins at d3:05:57:15 in Reel/Act 3

REL. TIME:

Columbo arrives on scene with his men to search the murder scene. He asks Frank a few questions about why Lester came back while explosives were set off . . . His men call out that they found something . . . Columbo displays a flashlight . . .

0:00			Begin music on CU Frank as he walks off in anger
2:84		CUT	dead man lying on gurney as Columbo approaches
4:54			bends down over body
5:41			looks at his collar
6:24			straightens back up
7:61			reaches into his jacket
9:31			pulls out a thin metal wand
17:92		CUT	CU Columbo's hand as he pulls back man's collar
18:32			to reveal a few leaves and twigs buried underneath
22:06			he carefully pulls them out with the wand
29:16			all onto the gurney . . .
30:03			VO: "Battalion's closed down until we find out why this accident happened . . ."
33:27			Pause in dial. Columbo poking around in collar
34:00		CUT	Group of soldiers sitting in bleachers/music out

REFERENCE:

34:73		Frank OS: "Last night we lost a comrade . . ."

TOTAL TIME – 34:00

END CUE 3m1

Note the capital letter A on the cue sheet; it refers to the size of the orchestra I was using. The first day of recording we used the A orchestra, and the next morning we had cut down to a smaller group, the B orchestra.

Page 1   4/18/89   3:20 A.M.

Word Games was the title of the two-hour movie for television that was the pilot for a series called "Mrs. Columbo."

The cue shown next, M-503, was done to a click track. The numbers following the timings on the cue sheet denote the beats of the track on which each timing falls.

The opening two measures and three beats convey an aura of mystery and ominousness that resolves into something a little lighter on the fourth beat of measure 3. This is where we see the exterior of Kate Columbo's house and the interior where she is working on a doorbell. The hard part here was to move gracefully from the "mystery" aura to something more neutral (the last beat of measure 3), then to brighten it up on the downbeat of measure 4. This was brought about by going from a G-minor ninth chord to a G ninth. The B-natural was all it took. Then, moving to the E-flat major seventh (a warm sound) set up the end of the scene and the beginning of the dialogue.

Note that there were seventeen clicks on the cue. As usual, the last chord was held out for an additional six or seven seconds to let the music die out naturally. The music mixer on the dubbing stage is the one who did the fade-out.

Some composers will not use a diminuendo on a music tail, assuming instead that it will be dialed out gracefully when the picture is dubbed. I find that chancy (unless you intend to be present while they're dubbing), because there's a slim possibility that it *won't* be faded out. Better to be safe than sorry. It is little things like this that make your score effective.

For some odd reason I did not title this particular cue. It was probably done later on by the music library staff at Universal who produced the show.

Music: Mrs. Columbo

John Cacavas   *clx 18.³*   Prod. #51901

WORD GAMES

REEL V – M-503

mm 78 +

After Kate and Norris go through Huston's house looking for the intercom, Norris says that there is no intercom in the Huston house and that the whole thing must be a coincidence. She thanks him, and he responds; "I understand, it's my pleasure." WHEREUPON

0:00.0		MUSIC BEGINS ON pause—TWO SHOT Kate and Norris
0:02.2	4	She turns and exits
0:04.3	6'/2	He exits down hall and WE PAN WITH him
0:08.4	12 CUT	EST. EXT. L.S. Kate's house—DAY
0:10.9	15'/2 CUT	M.C.U. Kate on ladder, turning screwdriver in doorbell
0:12.9	17'/2	MUSIC ENDS as she turns to the postman and says: "Try it again."
		END CUE

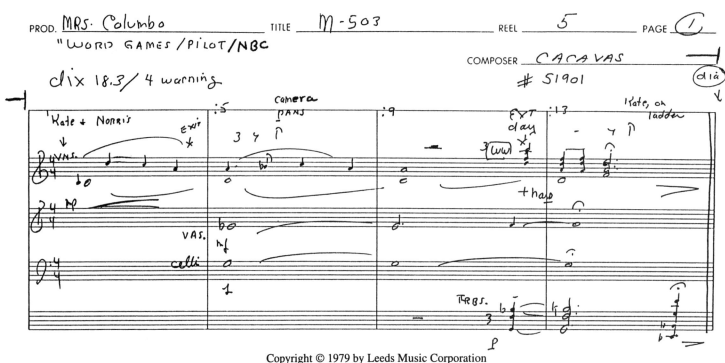

The next example, a cue from an ABC children's special, "Red Room Riddle," was done with a rather small orchestra, but was benefited by the help of two synthesizers. This particular cue, "The Red Room," was quite spooky. Because the feature was oriented toward children, I capitalized on the "spookiness."

The scene opened with a long shot of this haunted room. The use of all the low instruments injected it with the feeling of scariness. On the second beat of the third measure, we cut to a scene outside the house, with someone entering. Since the exterior setting was a sunny day, I altered the music somewhat to escape the scariness. The person was smiling, and I thought it might be a good spot to throw in a couple of bars of the main theme, which was English and folklike in character. However, we go back into the room on the fourth beat of bar 5 with dark, ominous harmony. The use of a rubbed gong and echo-plexed low instruments return us to the original mood.

The orchestra, by the way, consisted of four cellos, four violas, one bass, two synths, a piano, three woodwinds and two percussion.

In the film *Margaret Bourke White,* a situation arose that required me to compose some newsreel music from around 1940. The studio had licensed the actual newsreel footage, but it appeared that clearing the music behind it would have been too expensive and time-consuming. So what happens? Of course, the composer is called upon to replace the music, which in this case was not too difficult.

In the cue that follows, M-9M3, "Old-Fashioned Newsreel," I already had a standard dance band for one of my sessions in order to re-create many of the sounds of the 1930s and 1940s. It was performed in the style of the period. The saxes used vibrato on the unisons, and a kind of "pit band" theatrical tempo. Note that I broke up the trombones—two of them sustaining a harmony, and another playing muted along with the trumpets. This is not something I would usually do, but in this instance it didn't make any difference.

Before dubbing, it became necessary to eliminate all sound from the newsreel—meaning, in this case, the commentator's voice. The music track and commentator were "married" to the same track; therefore an actor was brought in to redo the commentary. Nothing is as simple as it seems.

I did not have to write an ending for the piece. As in the case of a lot of source music, it just went out in progress when the picture shifted to another scene.

BOURKE WHITE M-9M3

JOHN CACAVAS

The next example, from *Police Story II*, is a classic example of a short chase with a suspense section and the final denouement of the scene.

The orchestra was composed of two woodwinds (one being an EVI, or electronic voice instrument, which is capable of reproducing practically any instrument with only a few seconds needed for changeover), two horns, two trumpets, two trombones, piano, harp, guitar, two synthesizers, two percussion, violins, cellos and basses.

The chase starts off with a heavy, loud downbeat with agitated figures in the orchestra. In the middle of the third measure, there is a strong hit, which was a new camera angle on the speeding cars. In the middle of measure 5, the chase is over, and the police approach with drawn guns. The danger is over on the second beat of measure 8, and there is an ominous relaxation beginning in the middle of measure 9. The music fades out over dialogue. Note that the tonality stays practically the same for the whole cue.

As the entire cue was recorded to a click track, there was no need to place timings on the score. The timings and descriptions were placed on my sketch. I was given eight free warning clicks, and I was on my way. The dialogue entered in the middle of measure 10, and I made an especially long tail with a diminuendo. It would be dialed out gradually on the dubbing stage during the final mix of the picture.

In music of a nontonal nature, it is possible to score something without regard for harmonies as such. Sometimes referred to as "discrete" music, it consists more importantly of sounds and textures.

In the next example, from the film *Murder by Reason of Insanity*, the cue is a lead-in to the capture of the bad guy. The only real tonal sound is in the violas. A waterphone is employed, which provides an eerie background sound. The piano plucks random low strings, the cellos contribute a sliding pattern and the DX-7 and synthesized guitar do other unusual tricks.

A tonality of B-natural is established, however, which is further embellished in measure 3 when the cellos land on a low B. (The cellos are "tuned down" to achieve this note.)

When the guitar enters, you hardly hear the entrance because it involves a pedal that makes the sound come out of nowhere, via crescendo and diminuendo.

The middle of measure 3 reveals a subtle hit that just dies away. To make this music effective, one must not toss in too many things at the same time. As the cue progresses, the same sounds continue, but not necessarily in their original rhythmic patterns. For example, the flute pattern comes in once every three measures. The held note of the violas continues throughout the entire cue. This gives the music a kind of consistency. The basses, with their 16th-note figure (along with the synth), also sound every two or three measures.

The one thing this kind of cue does is create suspense with a tremendous amount of ominousness. The harmonies that emerge from the sounds, by their very nature of chance, are also very effective.

In the PBS production of *My Palikari*, the story concerns a Greek-American who returns to the land of his birth after a lengthy absence. The next cue, "The Arrival," is a series of camera shots of the Aegean Sea, mountains and a car winding its way through the mountain roads. It was a natural place to play the main theme of the picture—which is exactly what I did.

The melody (carried by the violins) is Greek in character and is further supported by the use of a bouzouki (a Greek mandolin-type instrument) and an accordion supplying typical "Greek dance" afterbeats. In the last half of measure 6, the car stops, and there is dialogue.

Because of the relatively low budgets of PBS productions, the whole picture was scored without projection, using a click track. Without clicks, it would have been impossible to score this picture in a four-hour session, which was what we did.

The orchestra was not large—nine violins, three cellos, one bass, a bouzouki (doubling a guitar), two woodwinds, two horns, harp, keyboard and two percussion.

The recording configuration was four-track tape (half-inch), three tracks of music and one track for the synch-pulse. This gave the music mixer some leeway during dubbing. We also ran a twenty-four track safety, which we fortunately did not have to go back to for remix. This was a common way of recording film music up until all the networks converted to stereo telecasting. The three-track music, by the way, was not stereo but simply triple-mono. (This allows the music dubbing mixer to raise and lower different sections, if needed.)

Writing music for "Columbo" was never easy, because of the ironic nature of the show. It contained a lot of tongue-in-cheek dialogue and lightheartedness as well as deadly serious topics. Things were never what they seemed, and it required a great deal of thought. Fortunately, I had a lot of help from the executive producer-writer Richard Alan Simmons. Not only was he a music lover but he also gave me a lot of hints and ideas about which way to go.

On the show "Grand Deceptions," there was a distinct military presence to the story. We decided to go with a main theme that was kind of martial, but with European overtones. This theme, which was used in the cue 6M1, was a natural for this scene. It consisted of a series of car-bys (cars driving by) and one of the characters, Mr. Dunstan, walking to his office on a military base. I used a "musette" accordion sound played by a synthesizer. The tuba accompaniment was not buffoonish but rather humorous. Now and then, I interpolated a bugle call–type passage. The drums were used sparingly, just enough to suggest soldiers. The show opened up, by the way, with a camera panning a mock battlefield with toy soldiers in various formations. At measure 13, wanting to change the color a little bit, I added an oboe and clarinet to the synth. If you examine the sketch carefully, you will find something always going on, but never too much. Although there are no dynamic indications on the sketch, everything was played softly and delicately—just the opposite of a blaring march. The orchestration was minimal, in keeping with the concept of toy soldiers. I did not use this music during the murder sequence but instead did a paraphrase as the murderer was cleaning up the mess afterward.

PROD. # 6410   TITLE 6 m1   REEL _____   PAGE 2

"Grand Receptions"

COLUMBO   COMPOSER JOHN CACAVAS

When we were spotting (the term used for determining the placement of music in a film) *Deadly Deceptions*, there was a sequence with a secretary running around an office, frantically looking for missing papers. It was funny in a way, but not hilarious. I was dreading the possibility that Richard Simmons would want a cue there, because I didn't have a clue as to what to do.

–He said: "What do you think?"

–I shrugged my shoulders hoping the whole thing would go away.

–"Pizzicato strings?" I asked hopefully.

–He made a face.

–"What about a kind of fugue of bugle calls?" he asked.

–I felt joy well up within me. I would never have thought of anything as daring as that.

–"I'll need another trumpet," I said.

–"Be my guest" was the reply, and off we went.

The fugue turned out just terrific, and an otherwise ordinary scene sprang to life. Sometimes as composers, we can't tell the forest from the trees, and we tend to be too conservative. A suggestion like the one Simmons made could only have come from a music lover—one not afraid to go against the grain.

Eischied was a detective series I scored for Columbia and NBC that was filled with action, as most cop shows are. The cue we're going to examine now is typical of the genre. We open with a serious situation, move to an establishing shot of the city and then into the squad room. In this case, the interior of the squad room is a humorous, light setting. For a 24-second cue we have three different kinds of material to play. The secret is to make it all blend and not sound disjointed. In other words, we are looking for a "flow" to create our cue.

The first three measures, with unison horns and cellos, give us our serious moment. In measure 3 we start our buildup with a crescendo, and at measure 4 we play the theme of the show. A neutral establishing shot is always a good place to play the theme. We hit the interior of the squad room on the last beat of measure 6, but I don't make a big thing out of it; it's just a natural ending of the theme. The remaining measures are not meant to be funny but rather light in nature with warm chords. Major sevenths fit the bill very well.

To recapitulate, we have scored something ominous, neutral and lighthearted in 10 measures, and basically it makes sense as one complete composition.

When I examined the full score to this sketch, I discovered that I added a light drum pattern to the theme, and a celesta doubling the woodwinds in measures 7, 8 and 9. By using the Fender Rhodes keyboard on the downbeats of measures 4 through 10, I was able to establish the harmony of each measure before the strings came in on the second beat.

Another thing to remember: this cue is really only a transition between two scenes; beyond the first three measures (which address the situation) the rest is bridge material.

By using a 2/4 measure at the beginning, the timing works out so that the main theme will occur on the downbeat of measure 4. Otherwise, it would have occurred on beat 3 of the measure, which would not be as effective.

MUSIC TIMING

Title of Production   Eischied The Demon, Part I   *TRANS*

Production #   183605   **Total Timing**   :23.9   *C/X 18.1*

Title of Cue

Sequence   M31   STARTS AT 431 FEET   5 FRAMES

PREV. SEQ. The ballistics expert has told Earl that the bullets from both killings match. Earl says IF YOU'RE RIGHT, WE HAVE A MASS-MURDERER ON OUR HANDS.

STRING! 1   :00.0   We are CU on the expert as he stares back at Earl.

:01.0 2'½ CUT   CU Earl; he blinks his eyes as he looks at the expert.

:02.75 4'½ CUT   F.S. Earl turns and leaves.

:05.5 8'½   Earl out of camera, it holds on stand containing guns.

:07.5 11   CUT   F.S. large bridge over the Hudson, camera panning toward the   skyscrapers toward police building.

15.9 22   CUT   Shooting through a door window, we see Alessi coming in with a cat in a carrying case and going through all the detectives at work.

:19.3 26'½   They all start to applaud him as he tries to be cool and continues walking by them, camera panning with him.

:23.9 32'½   Music tails here as Alessi speaks to Earl about his cat.

TOTAL TIME :23.9

Sometimes a dramatic climax is served better by eliminating the music rather than playing it. In a segment of "Kojak," I did just that. The heavy, played by Paul Anka, was stalking an adversary through a deserted, uninhabited old building. At first, the victim-to-be just walks, now and then furtively looking over his shoulder. He walks faster, panic-stricken, and finally reaches a dead end, an elevator shaft without the elevator. Anka comes up behind him, gives him a gentle shove and the man falls screaming down several stories to his death.

The sequence, which lasted about a minute, was a composer's dream as far as writing suspense music was concerned. Rather than build up to a climax and score the falling and screaming, I played it in silence. In other words, I let the screaming become the score. The example follows:

In this "Kojak" segment, I asked the engineer to give us a lot of room echo to convey the feeling of the deserted building. Sometimes it is safer to add the echo on the dubbing stage, but in this case I wanted to make sure it was done my way. I wanted the struck percussion and piano to sound very soft and distant, which the engineer did for me. At forty seconds, we add a soft string chord, which consisted of an A-major triad (with a flatted fifth) superimposed on an open-harmony C chord.

One would think that the low C would be the root, but E-flat worked a lot better. It was not muddy either, the low strings serving as an entity unto themselves.

Please note that as the bad guy gets closer to his prey, the bass notes get busier, the orchestra increases in volume and we add woodwinds and stopped horns. On the downbeat of the last measure, the man falls down the elevator shaft screaming. His scream starts exactly at the cutoff note of the orchestra.

By the way, the A chord over the C-major chord works quite well with a pure A-major chord, as opposed to one with the flatted fifth.

By not changing the harmony or bass notes, we can convey a feeling of suspense through the repetition. If a cue is not too long, this economy of notes always works. Another reason for keeping the music simple was the sound effects: I wanted the footsteps of the bad guy to be a part of the auditory experience. I also made sure that the "tempo" of the footsteps was different from my accented low notes. If they had matched, the effect would have been corny.

With the exception of two episodes, I scored all five seasons of "Kojak." Each week brought a different situation that required a different approach.

The producer, Jim McAdams, was extremely music-oriented, and we discussed how we would handle every show that we did. He was very much against "on the nose" musical characterizations or obvious solutions to our problems. For example, in "The Chinatown Murders," he was dead set against any gongs or funny Chinese sounds. In other words, he wanted the music to remain pure and address the scenes without being ethnic. Being deprived of those instruments made my work harder, but in the last analysis it made for a better score. As I said earlier, it was the communication between composer and producer that made things work properly.

The same could be said about my work with Bill Frye, the producer at Universal who gave me my first job in Hollywood and went on to hire me for many more films including the *Airport* series. He knew exactly what he wanted, and being very knowledgeable and artistic, he was a great help in fashioning my scores. I may also add that both these men could be ruthless on the dubbing stage. If one of my cues didn't work as well as expected, it would be tossed and replaced with nary a thought as to my bruised and bloody ego. They were right, of course. If something doesn't work, get rid of it. There are times when music doesn't really work in a scene. In those situations, the composer usually agrees to eliminate the offending morsels.

If a cue of yours is discarded, just remember that it isn't because they don't like you; it's that the cue doesn't work for that particular scene. Chances are, there is something else in your score that can replace it admirably.

The next cue, "Take-off Drama" from *Airport '77*, was designed to capture the excitement of the takeoff but still conveys the tension and danger with the intercuts of the bad guys. The tension relaxes a little at about 28 seconds, when we cut to the interior of the plane and dialogue. The danger is still present, though, so I did not alter it too much.

I had the advantage of a very large orchestra, and with the activity of the plane taking off, engine noises and all, the orchestra was used to full effect.

Harmonically, the cue is based on only one chord—A-minor with added B's, with the fifth fluctuating between the E and F, creating an augmented fifth. The bass constantly remained on a pedal A. There is no melody as such, only moving contrapuntal lines creating a pattern. The main thrust of the rhythm is given by the violas and cellos which continue during the action sequences. They relax during the dialogue and when we see the "heavies" revealed.

The climax of the cue is at beat 32, and the main theme is paraphrased in the next few measures. Shortly after this printed example, the cue fades out into dialogue.

Note that the different rhythms of the various contrapuntal lines create a kind of turbulence—never really dissonant, but unsettling nevertheless.

The 3/4 measure at the beginning was used to hit the climax (beat 32) on a downbeat.

Music: **Feature**

John Cacavas   Airport '77   Prod. #02092

Reel III – M-300 (Added Cue)

16.3 $dx\ 18.7$	The plane is situated in taxi position on end of runway. CAM. is situated over shoulder of pilot, looking out onto runway. Tower control states; "Two Three Sierra, you're cleared for takeoff." Gallagher states; "Roger, tower, understand, cleared for takeoff."
0:00.0	MUSIC STARTS AFTER ABOVE LINE, OVER INT. of cockpit, looking out over runway. Plane is stationary.
0:01.8 $3\,1/2$	CUT TO EXT. of front section of plane, LOW ANGLE, looking upward.
0:02.3 4	Plane starts moving.
0:05.4 8	CUT TO INT. from behind pilot, looking out onto runway.
0:06.1 $8\,1/2$	Gallagher: "We're rolling."
0:06.7 $9\,1/2$	END OF LINE
0:07.2 10	CUT TO EXT.—LOW ANGLE—of plane taxiing. CAM. FOLLOWS plane.
0:15.7 21	CUT TO INT.—on an M.C.U. of security guard, locked into his seat.
0:17.7 $23\,1/2$	CUT TO MED. SHOT of the two culprits, dressed as stewards. One is looking toward guard. CAM. SLOWLY AND CAUTIOUSLY MOVES IN.
0:20.0 $26\,1/2$	END OF ZOOM IN TO M.C.U. of the two hijackers.
0:20.4 27	Other one of the hijackers looks toward guard.
0:21.8 $28\,1/2$	CUT TO CU of guard looking straight ahead and concentrating on takeoff.
0:24.3 $3\,1/2$	CUT TO L.S. of plane leaving ground.
0:26.8 35	Plane comes into a M.S. and CAMERA PANS AND FOLLOWS it.
0:29.0 38	CUT TO INT.—M.C.U. of little girl and her mother.
0:29.6 $38\,1/2$	Little girl turns her head toward her mother. Little girl: "How fast can this plane go, Mommy?" -
0:31.9 $41\,1/2$	Mother: "Fast enough."
0:32.7 $42\,1/2$	END OF LINE. Little girl turns her head forward.
0:34.6 45	CUT TO M.C.U. of TV screen. Ground is FOLLOWED by the TV CAMERA.
0:43.6 $56\,1/2$	CUT TO M.C.U. of Benjy and his mother.
0:44.2 57	Benjy: "Grandpa sure has a neat plane, doesn't he, mom?"

The next example, from "Eischied," is a very dramatic, emotional cue for strings only. Where the parts are marked "intense," the strings really dig into it.

Note the dissonances that constantly resolve before a relaxing in the fourth measure. My notes show that we recorded it "wild" because the actual film wasn't available. Some minor problems were caught by use of accents; hence the click track was invaluable.

MUSIC TIMING

Title of Production Eischied (Part Two)　　(Warning Clicks 4　18.4

Production # 183605 **Total Timing** :16.1

Title of Cue Sequence M51 **Starts at** 197 Feet 09 Frames

Prev. Seq. Alvin drops his gun as he was ordered. Earl (stalking toward) HOW ABOUT TO BE IN THE OTHER SIDE　Alvin screams: DON'T SHOOT!

:00.0	End of line as camera stays on horrified face of Alvin.
:00.55 CUT	CU Earl's face moving closer to Alvin in FG, glaring.
:03.8 CUT	A detective jumps into the shot and grabs Alvin from his back and
:04.7	starts to handcuff him as camera stays on desperate Alvin's face.
:08.2 CUT	CU Earl glaring.
:11.1 CUT	CU Alvin staring back helplessly.
:12.9 CUT	Earl glaring .... yet we sense that Earl is feeling sorry for the killer.
:16.1 CUT	INT. of Police Headquarters as cops peeking through the blinds; the crowd, angered, outside .... as MUSIC tails.

PROD. Eischied (Pt II)   TITLE M-51   REEL 5   PAGE 1
183605
(clix 18·4)   " Earl Glares "   COMPOSER John Cacaln

Writing neutral music is never easy. Because music can evoke emotions, it is hard to write a piece that doesn't do so. In the following example, from a picture called *Dead Wrong*, the first part is an attempt to create neutralness and move into a kind of seriousness. The example is scored for violas, cellos, bass and woodwinds. It is very slow and just wanders, since there was dialogue over quite a bit of the score.

As for the timing technique, I just conducted freely to the stopwatch and had the music editor punch the film every eight seconds. If I reached a punch too soon, then I knew I was conducting a little fast, and would slow down. If I hit a punch late, then I would speed up. The punches, by the way, create a blinding flash of light in the darkened studio, so you can be looking at your score and not at the screen.

If I were recording "wild" with a picture, I'd surely write it to a 24.0 click track, which is one beat per second. It would still be possible, however, to record to the clock only, without any trouble.

Writing music for comedies—I don't mean cartoon-type pieces but music that actually underscores the humor and lightness in certain kinds of films—is not a simple proposition.

Classical music seems to work. Somehow, it kind of plays against the picture, without commenting on the film action.

I learned this when I was asked to score the television series "Four Seasons." Alan Alda wanted to use Vivaldi (which he also used for the feature motion picture), and so Vivaldi we used. I had to shorten certain pieces, creating endings and all that, but no matter what piece of his I used, it always seemed to work. It had a magical way of complementing the screen action no matter what direction it took. Somehow the very Baroqueness of the music, the transparent orchestration and straightforward melodies, made the whole thing a delight. Many pictures have used classical music—*Prizzi's Honor* and *A Little Romance*, for example, come to mind.

Once we started a piece on "Four Seasons," it would just play across all scenes, dialogue and changes of locale. I didn't alter the score, since I'm sure that would have brought a lot of irate letters. It should also be mentioned that the orchestra was ideal, just strings and harpsichord with an occasional wind instrument. We never had any problem with the music fighting the dialogue. So rather than try to be a joker with a humorous picture, go back to the old masters. They knew what they were doing.

Erma Levin, one of Hollywood's great music editors, told me a funny story.

It seems that a down-and-out trombone player had reached the point where he had to pawn his instrument. When he arrived at the pawn shop, a stuffed rat caught his eye.

"It's really quite clever," said the owner. "You see, you just turn it around and wind it up, and it moves."

The trombone player was entranced. "I'll take it," he said. "Just deduct the price from what you're giving me for the trombone."

He then took it outside and wound it up, and the stuffed rat started to move down the street. Soon other rats came out of nowhere and began following. Suddenly, there were hundreds of rats following the trombone player and the stuffed rat.

Eventually they came to the waterfront of the town, and the stuffed rat jumped in, followed by the hundreds of followers. Needless to say, they all drowned.

The trombone player could hardly believe it. He ran back to the pawn shop and asked the owner: "Do you have any stuffed synthesizer players?"

WRITING FOR DOCUMENTARY AND INDUSTRIAL FILMS

*A*long with student films, documentary and industrial filmmaking is the area where most young composers get their start. One basic difference between a dramatic television show or feature film and a documentary is the way the music is used. A documentary has what is known as "wall-to-wall" music, whereas most other films use music to underscore mood, action and dialogue.

Most of the music is under narration, and often the narration is not in place when the composer starts work. If this is the case, you must try to find out the gist of the narration for guidelines as to the kind of music to write. The only logical way to succeed is to make your music fit the film and leave the dialogue to the mixers on the dubbing stage. If the music "works" with the picture, then you have done your job well. It is also prudent to remember that you cannot second-guess the content or placement of the dialogue. Just assume it is going to be there, and treat it like a sound effect. The mixers on the stage will raise the volume of your music when there is no dialogue and lower it under the narration. A word of warning: if you score your picture too "thin" (i.e., if you are too concerned about narration), it will *sound* thin. The better it sounds on the playback during your recording session, the better it will sound underneath the effects and narration.

Usually your music recording budget is not as healthy as in a commercial film; therefore, you must choose your instrumentation wisely. Although it is possible to score a wildlife documentary with a flute, guitar and percussion, this trio would be woefully inadequate for a film extolling the noise and activity of a ball-bearing manufacturing plant or a steel mill.

With the countless number of synthesizers and other electronic instruments available to us, the palette is a lot broader than it was years ago. There are many documentaries scored solely with these instruments, and it's fine as long as you have your own studio, or access to one. Otherwise, you can go broke as a result of studio time and rentals associated with the vast amount of overdubbing and laying of tracks required by electronic recording. If you're going to go the electronic route, make sure you get a realistic idea of what the total bill will be. Since most documentary films are budgeted on a "package" basis, you might find yourself going in the hole.

Chances are, you won't be recording to projection, so you'll be able to record more music per hour than you could if you were scoring a picture. In order to attain split-second timing, it's advisable to record with a click track. That way, there will be no errors in timing. If the timing is not that crucial (in slow, rubato scenes, for example), then one could conduct with a stopwatch. However, with wild recording, the click track is foolproof.

If you have the time, you might consider creating alternate versions of the cues you are unsure of. Perhaps if something is too heavy you might want to thin it out, thus giving your producer or director some leeway or choices. He or she will love you for it.

When I was scoring the television series "Four Seasons" for Alan Alda and Universal, the underscore consisted totally of works by Vivaldi—cut down, of course, but still Vivaldi. Because the show contained only about seven minutes of music and we were allowed to record fifteen minutes for the session, I started to bring in alternate cues. As you can imagine, this made Mr. Alda quite happy, and he spent a lot of time on the dubbing stage tossing cues back and forth. Finally the studio asked me to stop recording the alternates because Alda was using too much dubbing time! That's show business, I guess. However, if you have the time, it is certainly worth considering.

> *Andre Previn recounts an incident that happened when he was at MGM. Irving Thalberg, the studio chief, heard something in a score that he didn't like, and was informed by an office minion that it was a minor chord. The next day Thalberg circulated a memo stating that "henceforth, there will be no more minor chords in MGM pictures."*

> *A similar experience befell the late Jerry Fielding when he was signed by producer Irwin Allen to score* Beyond the Posideon Adventure. *Allen's assistant called Fielding to tell him that Mr. Allen wanted "wall-to-wall" music and no discords in his picture.*

WRITING FOR PUBLICATION

So, you want to get a work of yours published. Why not? You've directed a high-school band, or you're a professional free-lance composer-arranger and feel that you can write works as good as what's out in the marketplace. Let's start with the concert band field, for example. First, you must decide the grade level for which you want to write, and next find out what kind of material is selling. You'll be up against a lot of competition—not only talent, but also names.

BAND PUBLICATIONS

I suggest going to a band music dealer first and obtaining copies of their top ten sellers in that category (not the whole sets, just the scores). Then, study them and find out why they are successful. Chances are, a recording might be available that will make your work much easier. A lot of these pieces might be arrangements of public domain material, and there might be several different versions offered by different publishers. The last thing you need is a rejection from a publisher who already has a version in print.

My suggestion is to write an original. You might also consult a dealer about what he or she thinks the market could use most—perhaps a small overture, a concert march or something else. Once you've decided on the kind of piece you're going to write, write it! First, do a sketch, taking into careful consideration the ranges, instrumentation (a young band might have a reduced instrumentation), keys and length.

The next step is to make your transposed full score. And then, if you are not an established writer, you will have to get a recording made, and that will require parts. Although copying your own parts can be a chore, it gives you another opportunity to correct errors and make changes that will enhance the piece.

Now you've got to get someone to record it. Your local high-school band—or better yet, a college band—is the obvious, and sometimes the only, choice.

See to it that your music is proofread, easy-to-read and written on good-quality music paper. Designate key signatures, dynamics and so on in red ink, which will save you time during recording. Once you've got your tape, take it to a recording studio for improvement in echo, equalization and anything else that might make it sound as good as possible. Remember, as an anonymous entity to a publisher, your tape can make or break you.

For submission to a publisher, I recommend a very neat copy of your condensed score (sketch) plus a cassette of the music along with an explanatory letter that is short and to the point. You are submitting this piece for publication. Period. No comments about how much the kids loved it, how you feel it would become a big hit and all that garbage. Don't forget to enclose a self-addressed, stamped return envelope. Not absolutely necessary, it's but a thoughtful touch.

Next, you must decide on the publisher to whom you're going to submit the work. Unfortunately, the list of educational publishers has dwindled in the last several years. The bright side is that you will find pretty much an open-door policy. They are interested in publishing the best material available, and if you've got something great, you'll most likely luck out. DO NOT LET REJECTIONS DISCOURAGE YOU. Often a publisher rejects something because the company does not have an open slot in that category. Too many marches on the schedule, for example. A piece of advice: do not submit the same piece to more than one publisher at a time. Although you might wait a long time for an answer, simultaneous submission is a no-no. It's a very tight business, and the last thing you need is bad word of mouth.

A professional does not let rejections stand in his or her way but constantly submits and resubmits material, always seeking out the best publisher for the project.

Many years ago, when I first entered the publication field, I wrote a choral work (something like an ersatz "Ghost Riders in the Sky") and received eleven rejections before it was finally accepted for publication—and not with great enthusiasm, I might add. The editor needed another piece to fill out his schedule, and I had submitted many works to him before (which showed him I was not a one-time composer). He felt that it might have some pop possibilities, so he decided to give me a chance.

Well, the piece was a big hit. It sold thousands and thousands of copies and is still around today. Never give up, that's the key.

While you are cooling your heels waiting for an answer, you must begin a new piece. Use a different medium, perhaps—or the same thing, but in a different grade level or category. Educational publishers are not particularly interested in one-time composers. It is very expensive to publish and promote, so they like to think their writers are serious about building a career.

Don't expect immediate riches once you get a piece published. In most cases, more than a year will elapse before you see a dime. The terms of the standard contract issued by a reputable publisher are 10 percent of the retail selling price. Anyone who offers you less is being very naughty.

Before you submit your work to a publisher, find out the name of the editor who is in charge. If you just send it to "Editor, XYZ Music" it may well be returned unopened. Again, a small effort, such as taking the time to find out the editor's name, is what distinguishes the pro from the amateur. It's also a good idea to write to the editor in advance, telling him or her to expect the submission. That way, when your music and tape arrive, they won't be a total surprise.

Assuming you get your work published, you'll be asked to proofread the printed score and parts. The publisher (in most cases) will also have engaged a professional proofreader, so there will be the additional protection of another set of eyes, and you'll be working from clean copies.

Take your time in going through everything very carefully. Do not rush. Once it's printed, the music is cast in stone, as they say, and changes are impossible. It is there forever unless it becomes very successful and goes into another printing (which means you'll have a second chance). But don't count on that. Do it carefully the first time.

You will be asked to provide program and performance notes for your publication. Sometimes I find these harder to write than the music. The performance notes are directed at the conductor and should include your thoughts about tempo, conception and so on—anything that will help achieve a better performance. The program notes need to be something that could also appear in a concert program and be of interest to the audience. If your piece is an arrangement of a classical work, then of course you want to include something about the composer, such as when it was written and anything else that gives the audience a better sense of the work.

You won't be asked for any input on the cover of the publication, but you will be asked for some biographical material and a photo. Make sure they are both first-class.

Several years ago I wrote a concert march called "Their Finest Hour," under the nom-de-plume of Theodore Maki. (Theodore Maki was a Greek resistance fighter against the Nazis in World War II and had a connection with my family.) I recorded the piece in London with a wonderful group of British studio musicians, along with four other works for band. Because we had budgeted for one three-hour session, we did not have time to dillydally around. It would have been nice to spend more time on the nuances, but to tell you the truth, I was relieved just to have gotten the pieces recorded with a decent balance and without mistakes.

The works were published, and miniature scores were mailed out along with a recording of the music. A couple of months later, the publisher forwarded to me a letter from a very irate band director complaining about the way John Cacavas had conducted this most wonderful concert march by Theodore Maki. He went on to pinpoint several small problems with the recording, and it was obvious that this gentleman had done his homework.

I wrote back to the man as John Cacavas, saying I appreciated his most informative letter, and took note of his various criticisms. I also told him that I had not heard a word from Theodore Maki, and therefore he could have not been too displeased with the recording. I also remarked that the royalty checks on "Their Finest Hour" would be quite healthy, and perhaps that's why Mr. Maki was keeping silent. I finished by telling him that when one has to record over twenty minutes of music in a three-hour session (with twenty minutes for a break), nervousness sometimes overtakes artistic integrity.

I never heard from him again, thank God. I lived in fear that every time I recorded something he'd write to me again, giving me bad grades. There are times when compromises must be made, but the secret is to keep them as small as possible, lest you get irate letters.

If you are going to pursue the career of a published composer, there are other instrumental combinations to consider. Collections of clarinet quartets, for example, or flute trios and brass ensembles, can offer substantial rewards. Whereas band publications seem to have their strongest sales in the first year after publication, instrumental collections have a longer shelf life. Some of my collections are still selling moderately well after being published twenty years ago.

It stands to reason that the market will absorb more simple arrangements than difficult ones. However, you can still be clever when writing for a simpler medium. As before, your music dealer can give you a lot of hints in this area. In my personal experience, a book of flute trios sold best, followed by the clarinet quartets.

You would probably have a tough time getting a book of bassoon trios published, but a book of bassoon solos with piano accompaniment would be an easier sell.

The solo instrument field (with piano accompaniment) is very specialized but one worth attempting. It's wise to present a graded series to a publisher covering about three levels of difficulty, and perhaps four instruments, to start with. If you do attempt this kind of project, the piano parts will be very important. If you're not a pianist, consult with one while you are writing. Usually the piano parts can be more advanced than the solo part. A little hint: the piano part should contain an extra staff above it for the solo instrument cue (in concert pitch, of course).

As far as the strings go, solos can have a good sales potential. String quartets are next to impossible to get published (unless you are recognized as a serious composer) because of the great amount of classical literature available. But just remember that many states have music contests, and the solo categories always need new material. You might check one of the state contest lists to see what is being chosen. It will guide your decisions.

Don't be afraid to use your connections. A music buyer for a dealer knows who is in charge at the various publishing firms, and that person has a lot of power. No publisher in his or her right mind would dare alienate a buyer. If there is no music buyer in your area, go to a nearby city, find one to take out to lunch and pick that person's brains. Music buyers have an immense amount of knowledge regarding the business and can save you a lot of trouble in the long run.

Attend music conventions. The large firms are usually represented at clinics and conferences and have booths displaying their publications. There is no better way to meet the staff of these companies, especially the salespeople, who are usually in attendance. After all, without the salespeople, your material could very well end up in a vacuum.

You might consider asking a published composer to recommend you to a particular company, assuming you are friends or associates. As with many other areas, who you know counts.

Regarding the copyrighting of your material, there are two schools of thought. For an instrumental or choral work, I don't think it is likely that a publisher will steal your material. For that reason, I never copyright my works. Songs are a different matter, though. A simple © at the bottom of the manuscript will suffice. And remember that if you copyright a piece and don't get it published until three years later, it is that much closer to the public domain.

The most efficient way to copyright your material is to send it to the Library of Congress with the appropriate form and fee. However, it is not necessary to do all that for a copyright. It only helps in matters of lawsuits or infringement cases.

I don't think it is necessary to write to publishers just to ask if they'd be interested in your work. They might not answer, and then what? It's better just to send the darned thing off. Most publishers are interested in seeing new material, since a hit can come from anyone. Just make sure you keep a log of what you are sending, both to whom and when. If you don't hear anything after a few weeks, there is nothing wrong with sending a reminder.

In closing, just remember one important thing: do not get discouraged when you receive a rejection! Just keep writing and submitting your work. In time, a publisher just may take you seriously. As a composer, one must develop a thick skin and be able to take a few heartbreaks. Being a creative person is asking for trouble. But you'll also get a lot of satisfaction, pride and, if you're lucky, a lot of money. There is nothing better than making money while you're asleep. Just ask a banker.

ORCHESTRA PUBLICATIONS

Getting music for orchestra published presents a whole new set of problems. Again, unless you are in the major leagues with recordings of your works and in demand with commissions, the market for orchestral works is limited. Most schools' string programs have diminished—and, along with them, the budgets for new music.

There are several experts in the field who arrange the classics for young orchestras, although it is entirely possible for new writers to break in. One must be extremely literate about what young string players are capable of, not to mention able to put it down on music paper. Most publishers realize that sales will be smaller in comparison to those for concert bands, for example, and therefore they release fewer new orchestral works. One alternative is to try to write a better arrangement of something that has already been successful. This requires research into the marketplace (speaking to the dealers, naturally) and attendance at orchestra clinics, where one can get a feel for what's happening out there.

I don't mean to discourage a composer from writing an original piece and submitting it. Since there are not that many orchestras around, it will be harder to get a demonstration record, but not impossible. And you never know until you try. Maybe the youth-orchestra world is ready for another *Bolero*, who knows?

If you've written an orchestral work that is lengthy and difficult, you might consider submitting to a publisher for rental, which means furnishing a complete set of well-copied and legible parts plus a full score. The publisher will then include the work in its rental catalog. This may or may not result in some rentals. It's up to you to create a demand for the music, either by mail or by word of mouth. A great deal of our contemporary orchestral literature today is available only on rental. Needless to say, it's a tremendous advantage to have a good recording of your work. Not only will it aid prospective performers but it will assist in the proper performance of the work.

None of this is easy, but if you have faith in your work it is well worth the investment of time and money.

If you're going to tackle something for youth orchestra (for publication), you should be aware of several things. First of all, in addition to a full score, a piano-conductor part is usually required. As in the days of Bach, it helps to fill in a less-than-adequate instrumentation. Next, be sure to include three saxophone parts (two altos and a tenor). Although they are optional, they are included for safety purposes. Sometimes a substitute viola part is written for violin III. This presents a range problem, so obviously it has to be adjusted here and there. I would be a little leery of things like an English horn solo. Make sure you cue it elsewhere. Even an oboe solo could be cued for a clarinet.

It goes without saying that the violins must not go too high. Give the part an octave lower too, for those who'd rather play it safe.

The instrumentation is as follows: two flutes, two oboes, two clarinets and one bassoon, three trumpets, three trombones, four horns (I usually write just two horn parts, since that's probably all you're going to get), percussion (three players, tops), piano, conductor and the three saxophones. You can also include a tuba part, which should be optional. And the strings, of course, along with the violin III/viola part.

I have seen many works for young orchestra with smaller brass sections, such as two trumpets and two trombones, but I would opt for the full sections.

The younger the orchestra, the safer you must make the work. This is not a place to which you want to limit yourself, but it is a viable market. The experts who specialize in this field do very well.

> *After the success of* Gallant Men, *recorded by Senator Dirksen, many other famous personalities asked us about the possibility of making a spoken word recording. Among them was Robert Kennedy and the then mayor of New York, John Lindsay. For one reason or another, none of them happened.*
>
> *Arch Lustberg, who had been working at ABC as a producer, had come over to Chappell Music at my request and was spending a great deal of time on our recording projects. Charles Osgood, the famed radio and television personality, was the third member of our group. We spent a lot of time drumming our fingers on a table . . . waiting.*
>
> *And then came the famous six-day war between Israel and the Arabs. It was either Arch Lustberg or Charles Osgood who came up with the idea to do an album with General Moshe Dayan. Now there was a hero! The war was only three days old when we decided to make our pitch to the general. But how? He was on the battlefield; we couldn't just write him a note or call him. Or could we?*
>
> *I was discussing our dilemma with Louis Cowan, the former president of CBS Television, with whom I had become friendly. He agreed that making contact would be difficult if not impossible, but all of a sudden he had an idea. Why not use the radio-telephone at CBS? They had people there in the field, after all. It was certainly worth a try.*

Cowan finally got through—not to the general himself, but to an aide. His name was Avi Har, and after some hurried conversations with Dayan, he determined that Dayan would love to do an album (Cowan told us later that he could hear bullets whistling and bombs going off).

We were ecstatic, already calculating the royalties. Then the other shoe fell. Yes, the general would be interested, but what kind of a cash advance were we offering? And perhaps we should be dealing directly with his agent, the William Morris office.

William Morris?

Three days earlier the world had never heard of General Moshe Dayan, and now he was signed with William Morris? The power and lure of show business—totally unreal!

Although we were just a little discouraged, we decided to pursue the matter, not with his agent but with Mr. Avi Har, or perhaps someone else.

Well, Mr. Avi Har thought that $25,000 was a reasonable advance. We decided to pass. And Moshe Dayan never made an album—at least none that I ever heard about.

RECORDING

When you listen to a live performance such as that of a symphony orchestra, are you hearing it in mono or stereo? The answer is mono, and the reason is quite simple: you are hearing the music from a single source. Although the brass may be on one side and the strings on another, there is still only one sound source. However, a stereo recording separates the sources into two channels (sometimes more), which results in what we call the "stereo" or "binaural" sound. That is probably why recordings often sound more precise and spatial than a live performance. I'm sure I'll get a lot of flak by saying that, but I believe it's true. Also, it is easy to enhance the room sound by artificial reverberation (for instance, when a recording is being made in a dead concert hall) and by utilizing various types of equalization that enhance the total sound.

This chapter will deal with recording in a rudimentary way, mainly via hints on achieving a better sound when recording educational organizations' performances. Recorded sound has come a long way since a single microphone hung in front of a group, and one just hoped for the best. We now have at our disposal DAT recording, which makes for a much cleaner sound by using the digital process. It also eliminates quality loss in moving from one generation to the other, which is unavoidable with tape or standard cassette recording.

It is true that professional multimiking is not the norm in most schools' recording facilities, but wonderful results can be achieved by hanging two microphones in front of the group while it is performing. The height of the mikes will vary from hall to hall, but after a little experimentation, the optimum position will make itself evident.

With most orchestral recording, the sound mixer is not as harried as, say, the mixer for a rock-and-roll recording. The balances tend to emanate from the performance, and the engineer need not raise the level when the band or orchestra is playing pianissimo. After all, that's the way it is *supposed* to sound.

If extra microphones are available, they probably should be used to bolster the flutes and such instruments as the bassoon or English horn. If there is a vibraphone part, it should also be boosted with a mike. Semiprofessional mixing panels can handle this without any problem. Naturally, if you are recording a choir along with your group, they will need separate microphones, and there should probably be some kind of separation to help in the mixing. When I say "mixing," I use the term guardedly. When one is recording on direct two-track stereo, no mixing takes place later. Maintaining some separation, however, makes it easier for the engineer to control things.

Because most schools' recording equipment does not include all the facilities for proper addition of echo or reverb, it's sometimes advisable to take the tape to a professional studio for the finishing touches. Certain techniques in equalization—brightening up certain things, perhaps adding bass and many other tricks of legerdemain—can improve the sound of your recording.

If you are lucky enough to have a hall blessed with a warm, rich concert-hall sound, then you may have to do very little. It has been my experience that there are very few of these halls around. They are usually too dead or too echo-filled. If the room is too live, then rugs, baffles and such can be placed here and there to help soak up the reverberating sound. Whereas too little echo will make a recording sound small and tinny, too much will make everything swim.

Many school bands, orchestras and choirs make recordings with limited pressings. There are several companies that will take care of the whole package, supplying the artwork and jackets for CDs and cassettes. They also claim to equalize the recording, and although some of these companies may have updated equipment to do so, most do not. Play it safe and take your recording to a studio that has the proper facilities to do it. Besides, you'll be able to hear the finished product before it goes to press. You won't be sorry.

A great deal has been written and discussed regarding the level of sound during playbacks. Years ago, engineers set what was considered a good and proper level, one that was between earsplitting and moderate. However, loudness always seemed to be equated with excitement. So now and then the monitors were raised against the engineer's wishes.

Then rock and roll, with its electronic gear, changed all that. Often the groups brought their own engineer, and the playback levels became deafening. Somehow these kids thought that the louder it was the better it was.

On the other hand, if the playback level is too soft, you might miss mistakes that otherwise would be heard at a higher playback level. A suspect inner voice, perhaps, or a wrong acoustic guitar chord might be lost to the ear if the monitor is too low.

I remember Leonard Bernstein telling me that whenever he played a recording of a certain piano concerto (in which he was the soloist) for guests, he always cleared his throat when a certain passage occurred that contained a mistake in his performance. He went on to say that it was not an obvious error, but it was not the way Beethoven wrote it. I asked him how the mistake got by, and he told me he was talking to someone, and the playback level was obviously too low. Needless to say, he cranked it up in subsequent recording sessions. In those situations where a control room is not available, and the equipment is set up in an area near the stage, playbacks are more critical because of the general commotion in the hall. Play it back good and loud so you won't miss anything.

Another common error in school recording is that the recording level is often too low. When the recording is then mastered, the sound level has to be pushed up, which means that tape hiss and noise will also be picked up. It is a good idea to test levels at the high end of the spectrum before recording. Whenever you have to push your volume up to an extreme when playing a recording, that means it was recorded at too low a level to begin with, or a mistake was made in mastering.

With the advent of rock and roll in the middle to late 1950s, jazz and swing music entered a period of decline that persists to this day. The big-name swing bands such as Tommy Dorsey, Benny Goodman and Harry James hit their stride in the late 1930s and 1940s, although jazz bands, ragtime and blues preceded that period for several years. After World War II, the public's enthusiasm for this music began to wane, and soon the era of singers was upon us. Perry Como, Frank Sinatra and Bing Crosby, among many others, had their own weekly radio and television shows, and the big bands began to disband. There were also vocal groups such as the Four Lads, the Four Aces and so on, who had their share of hit records. Elvis Presley and the Beatles became huge sensations, which effectively signaled the end of an era that today is a mere shadow of what it used to be.

Benny Goodman managed to hang on, although he was frustrated at the lack of interest in his kind of music. He was extremely versatile, not only as one of history's greatest jazz clarinetists but also as a fine performer of classical works. He managed to juggle the two idioms to great critical acclaim. Nevertheless, he brooded constantly about his lack of activity. During this time, he confided in his friend Morton Gould, with whom he shared a social and professional relationship. In addition to being a celebrated composer and conductor, Gould was a gifted pianist, and the two performed often in impromptu gatherings at their homes.

"Nobody wants me; nobody ever calls," complained Goodman.

Gould felt that this could not be the case, so he called the manager of one of the major symphony orchestras in the Midwest and said that Goodman might be available for a series of concerts with that organization. The manager replied by saying that they would love to have him; they had tried in the past but Goodman was always busy.

It was established that the manager would get in touch with Goodman and set up some engagements.

Weeks later Gould and Goodman were together again, and Benny was off on his usual tirade. He felt he was finished professionally. His band was disbanded, he was not being considered for solo engagements and so on.

"But weren't you contacted by the manager of the Pittsburgh Orchestra? I know for a fact that they want you," said Gould.

Goodman thought a moment. "Oh yeah, they did call me. But who the hell wants to go out there?"

PERFORMING RIGHTS SOCIETIES

*T*here are two major performing rights organizations in America: the American Society of Composers, Authors, and Publishers (ASCAP) and Broadcast Music, Inc. (BMI). There is also a third organization called SESAC, but it is only a very minor player in comparison to ASCAP and BMI. Since I have never met a composer who belonged to SESAC and have limited knowledge about the organization, I am not qualified to address it, so this section will deal with ASCAP and BMI.

A performing rights organization exists to negotiate license fees with the users of music, to collect those license fees and to distribute those fees in the form of performance royalties to the writers and publishers whose licensed musical works are performed in the media. By "performance" royalties, I mean primarily performances on television, radio, in concert halls and in bars, restaurants, roller skating rinks and the like. Both ASCAP and BMI have reciprocal agreements with performing rights societies throughout the world to collect their members' royalties from those societies.

Obviously these societies cannot log every performance played over the air, performed in a piano bar, or given at a local high-school band concert. Although the networks and certain cable and local television stations are logged 100 percent, other venues of performance are sampled. In the case of commercial establishments using music, the license fees collected in this area are, in the main, distributed on the basis of a writer's and publisher's radio and television feature performances.

Local broadcasting stations (both television and radio) are surveyed by means of audio and visual taping, through TV guides, TV data, newspaper listings and so on, and surveyed performances in these media are paid to writers and publishers on a quarterly basis.

ASCAP and BMI periodically negotiate with networks, cable companies and independent stations to determine license fees. Establishments such as restaurants and nightclubs pay an annual fee based upon established factors (seating capacity, type of entertainment, cover charge, etc.), which are applied uniformly throughout the country.

No royalties are collected for performances of music included in films being shown in U.S. theaters, although when these films are shown on television or cable stations, performance royalties are paid. Many of the foreign societies do collect license fees from motion picture theaters.

In recent years, both ASCAP and BMI have become more public relations–conscious and have instituted some worthwhile programs. They sponsor songwriter and theater workshops in addition to a film and television workshop. You need not be a member to apply for these workshops. They are extremely well run, and, having observed many of them, I can attest to their value. Unfortunately, you must live in either New York or Los Angeles to take advantage of them.

ASCAP has certain monies set aside each year for special awards to composers, songwriters and lyricists whose works have unique prestige value for which adequate compensation would not otherwise be received or are frequently performed in media not surveyed by ASCAP. Ballet, chamber works, college performances and educational films fall in the "standard" category. In the popular awards category, Broadway, off-Broadway, and resident theater, cabaret and other such venues would be covered. Awards are given by a committee of recognized professionals based on applications submitted by the members. Once a member reaches a certain plateau in regular performance royalties, he or she is no longer eligible for an award. It is ASCAP's way of rewarding talented writers whose works do not fall in the general area of commercial performance.

There are certain differences between the makeup of ASCAP and that of BMI. ASCAP is a membership association with all its income, less operating costs, being divided fifty-fifty between the writer and publisher members.

BMI is a privately held corporation and, unlike ASCAP, its total income and expenses are not a matter of public record. Whereas ASCAP may pay better in some areas and BMI in others, it is up to the individual to make the decision as to which organization to join. Once you have joined, you may resign if you are dissatisfied. With ASCAP, you may resign at the end of any year on three months' advance written notice. With BMI, you may terminate only by providing notice within a specific "window" period prior to the end of the two-year writer contract. Another point to consider is that ASCAP is owned by its writer and publisher members, whereas BMI is owned by radio and television broadcasters.

My advice to any person wishing to affiliate him- or herself with one of these two organizations is to send for material that explains the setup of each organization and to speak to various members for their advice and experience.

Both ASCAP and BMI base their royalty distributions on surveys of performances of various media. Some of these surveys are on a census (100 percent pickup), whereas others are conducted on a sample basis. If you get performances in an area that is sampled, there is a possibility that you might not get paid if you are on a local station that happens not to get surveyed. That can be discouraging, but if these societies were to pay on every television or radio play, there would be no money left for the members to share. It would all go to the logging expenses.

For those people engaged in writing for publication, all the American publishers today have both ASCAP and BMI companies. Recent years have brought many logged performances of educational band and orchestra music from abroad. Norway, Sweden and Japan are leaders in this area. More and more American symphonic band pieces are being recorded abroad, and they do get broadcast on radio. They are then logged by the local performing rights society, and the royalties are remitted to ASCAP for distribution. It does take a little time, though. One must figure anywhere from one to two years for payment, depending on which country is remitting. If something of yours gets played in Bulgaria or Borneo, don't hold your breath.

Many years ago, it was quite difficult for an ASCAP writer member to collaborate with a BMI counterpart. These difficulties were eliminated in 1972, and collaborations no longer present any problems. To facilitate the collaboration, the publisher splits the copyright between his ASCAP and BMI firms according to the writer split on the song.

It should be noted that musical theater works do not fall under the "small rights" category (e.g., songs, film scores, instrumental and vocal pieces) but rather under a category defined as "grand rights."

These performance royalties are negotiated between the producer and the composer-lyricist for these works and are a part of the running expenses of the musical. However, when these works are performed on radio, television or an orchestral/vocal concert performance (excerpts without dialogue), then they qualify for "small rights" performance and will be surveyed as such.

Educational, recital and concert performances are surveyed by the societies, but in a smaller way than the European societies. Many symphony orchestras (those licensed by ASCAP and BMI) send in their programs, and credit is given to the parties concerned. Certain colleges and universities have taken out licenses, and when the societies receive notification or programs of these events, those works also receive credit. However, it should be noted that with the exception of network television, local television and radio, BMI has no specific payment formula for any of the other licensed vehicles such as recitals or educational performances. Any distributions in these areas are made at the discretion of the BMI board and management.

Certain networks like PBS, A&E, Lifetime and so on, are surveyed on a sample basis. The royalties, compared to those of NBC, CBS and ABC, are considerably smaller because of the size of the license fees paid by these users relative to the three major television networks.

The ASCAP weighting rules and formula set forth the crediting formulas for all different types of uses (background music, themes, visual vocals, etc.). These formulas determine the number of credits each type of performance generates. These credits are then translated into "performance" dollars. One of the factors involved in arriving at the final dollar payment for a performance is whether the performance was a sampled performance (one pickup represents more than one performance) or a census performance. The weighting formula also applies to the crediting of concert and serious works performed in concert halls. However, even with this weighting system, the amount of money received for a performance won't be large, because the total amount collected in this area is small. The societies are constantly attempting to improve their logging capabilities, and the task is formidable when one considers the proliferation of cable channels that has become part of the broadcast tapestry. As more channels arrive on the scene, it means more logging and, with it, more expense.

Unfortunately for the writers and publishers, these new companies have seen fit to go to court to avoid paying royalties. They seem to subscribe to the philosophy that music should be free. ASCAP and BMI are constantly in court battling with these companies in an effort to set fair and reasonable license fees for the creative community. And, any guesses about where the money comes from to litigate? From the royalties that would otherwise go to the creators and publishers of the music, of course. It is not only the cable companies that are pursuing litigation. At one time or another, every network and independent television has been, or is, battling in the courts with ASCAP and BMI.

From the time of Beethoven, Bach and even earlier, it has been a constant battle for writers of music and words to receive their just compensation. One hopes that the future will bring more enlightened times for the people who devote their lifetimes to the creation of music.

The large rewards from the societies basically come to you if you are writing hit songs, have a long-running television series or write the scores to motion pictures. However, more and more royalties are coming from educational sources that were nonexistent years ago. As the surveying of concert and educational performances expands, perhaps more writers in these fields will be compensated.

During my tenure at Chappell, as director of publications in New York, I made periodic trips to the West Coast for composer meetings.

On one occasion I went to see Ira Gershwin with some new demos of his lyrics, which had been married to some unpublished Jerome Kern songs. We headed to the rear of his living room, whereupon he opened a small closet that revealed a record player. It looked quite beat-up and was probably older than I was at the time.

"Ira," I said, "there are a lot of new stereos on the market that would fit very well in this closet—cheap, too."

He looked at me, with the ever-present cigar in his mouth, and said, "It only takes one speaker to hear the words."

Touché.

AN INTERVIEW WITH MORTON GOULD

I think it can be stated truthfully that most of what we learn as composers and arrangers we learn from trial and error. It is one thing to be taught music, but it is something else to write it down and hear it performed. More and more university music departments are recognizing the need for laboratory situations as they are realizing that theory is one thing, practicality, another.

In my particular case, it was writing four-measure passages for my student jazz band and running the things down before a dance job. Finally, I assimilated enough information to be able to make an arrangement. Writing music is a constant learning process, no matter how gifted you may be. Each piece you write and hear played gives you experience that you will not get any other way.

Another way to get this experience is to work with someone who is better than you are. I was very lucky in that respect, having been able to work with Morton Gould as an orchestrator when I got out of the army. As I remarked in my book *Music Arranging and Orchestration,* I learned more looking over Gould's shoulder in two weeks than I learned in four years of college. I learned how to write things that *worked.*

What we were working on was going to be either recorded or published, so there were no second chances. It had to be right the first time.

I interviewed Gould for *Score,* the publication of the Society of Composers and Lyricists. The interview presents an overview of an extremely talented man of music, and I thought it appropriate that it be reprinted in this book. Working for him was a lucky break on my part, to be sure. However, I suggest you listen to his recordings, both his serious orchestral works and his timeless arrangements of America's popular music. You will learn a great deal, especially if you buy or rent the scores that go with them.

John: Unlike Europe, where so-called serious composers have always considered film compositions another form of expression, American composers have never really embraced the medium. Aside from you, Leonard Bernstein and Aaron Copland, for example, scoring films seems not to have been a popular endeavor. Would you like to comment on this?

Morton: I don't know why there has been a separation between composers who write for film and composers who don't. The fact is that a creative expression is a creative expression whether it is applied to film, to a concert or to an abstract piece. It's interesting to reflect that some of the great European composers (obvious examples like Prokofieff, Shostakovitch, Auric and Walton) had been writing for films as part of their creative expression. That really has not happened in this country.

John: People get typed.

Morton: Yes. And if you do something for even one film, you tend to get typed as a so-called Hollywood composer, whatever *that* means. On the other side is to be typed as a so-called serious composer, whatever *that* means. Certainly as far as I'm concerned, creating music on many different levels and of many different genres and for many different reasons is part of the excitement and fantasy of making music.

John: I remember in Hollywood years ago David Selznick asked Igor Stravinsky to do a score for a film, and Stravinsky sent the film back and suggested to Selznick that he write a score and they shoot a film to the score. He had a lot to learn about Hollywood!

To my way of thinking, your score to the miniseries "Holocaust," which was on NBC some years ago, was one of the finest scores ever created for television. The producer of that series was the late Herbert Brodkin. For all his awards and accolades, he was never regarded as being sensitive to music or to its use in film. What was your experience?

Morton: Well, my experience with Herb was that he was a very imaginative producer. I think he was slightly suspicious of what the music was going to do to his film. I really didn't have too many problems with him. In the case of "Holocaust," the only thing that disturbed me was that they took much of the music out. Hazards of the trade, and not an uncommon occurrence.

John: Thank God it was saved on the soundtrack album.

Morton: I think some of it, as we know, was. Composers always feel that their music shouldn't be touched. I never had that feeling.

John: I think that many directors are not particularly friends of composers. I think producers, however, see the broad picture (especially in television). And the director sometimes sees music interfering with dialogue and things like that.

Morton: Obviously he felt that. I do feel that there were a number of musical sections that I think were really part of the fabric and would have been of benefit.

John: Absolutely, I agree with that. Morton, you composed the scores to the "Cinerama" series of films, including *Cinerama Holiday* and *Windjammer*. Both were highly innovative. I remember particularly in *Windjammer* the opening scenes

were on a small screen, recorded in mono. When the screen went wide with those three cameras on the opening shot of the ship, the orchestra suddenly came out in stereo, full-blown. It was a wonderful moment—probably one of the great musical moments, in my opinion, on film. Could you tell us something about the assignment now?

Morton: I did not conduct those. They were conducted by Jack Shaindlin, who was very good and wonderful at getting things done. He had one of the greatest orchestras ever assembled. There is an example of filmmaking that was very much tied in with the music. And it was a real partnership by the very nature of those pictures and of "Cinerama." I had a great deal of freedom writing music that I think stands on its own. One funny thing that I do remember about *Windjammer* was that it went to different Caribbean ports. I said to the producer at one point, "Will you stop going to these tropical ports because I'm running out of tropical-influenced music! Get me up north."

John: Looking back during those days at Chappell Music in the late 1960s when your company was part of the Chappell group, one could say that those were really the golden years of standard and serious music publishing. Since the conglomerates have taken over the industry and farmed out a lot of their publishing, I don't think it's been for the better.

Morton: Individual music publishers have more-or-less disappeared, with a few exceptions. Many catalogs have been gobbled up, digested, ingested and redigested, and in some cases even disappeared for a while. With the advent of photocopying, the whole technology of publishing has changed. There is no doubt in my mind that for the individual composer it has been a difficult time, because in a way much of the music production that brought income is no more. We are living in an age of great technological developments. I think there is a big improvement over the way things were done in the past, but it has brought its share of problems.

John: During the early sixties you composed the score for the CBS documentary series "World War I." I remember learning an awful lot just looking over your shoulder. There was wall-to-wall music, and I don't recall your using any particular devices such as streamers, punches or click tracks. Just timings—and everything hit just perfectly. Would you like to elaborate on this?

Morton: I suppose I was just lucky. We worked under tremendous pressure for 26 weeks, as I recall. The conductor was Alfredo Antonini. When I'd finish, we would run the moviola. Alfredo and I were very conscientious about seeing that the timing was precise, because we didn't have any overtime for corrections if it didn't work. We were on a very tight budget.

John: It was amazing, because I remember seeing the scores and many, many bars go by, and all of a sudden I'd see something like 40.66 seconds. And I remember at the time there were no streamers on the film, and Alfredo hit it right on every time.

Morton: In a way it was more credit to him than to me. I really have a very special personal affection for that whole series. It has to do not only with the music but with what that period evoked. Now you and I are talking at the end of the century, and that was a series that visualized the beginning of the century through the First World War. If you recall, that [series] used a lot of archival film that dated back to the end of the last century to the beginning of this century.

John: And it's still being played on television today; that's the great thing about it.

Morton: Robert Ryan narrated the script, and there was no sound at all. It had to be carried by the music. I enjoyed doing it because of the generation that I come from; it's my early childhood and the first sounds I heard that I remembered.

John: As president of ASCAP and a prolific composer constantly doing major commissions and appearing as a guest-conductor with our top symphony orchestras, you're wearing a lot of hats. Is it difficult to juggle things?

Morton: Well I'm wearing a lot of hats and yet I'm bald . . . at least the top of my head is bald. It's very difficult to juggle things, except I've been doing this my whole life in one form or another. Don't forget, I spent many years doing weekly and sometimes twice-a-week radio programs. And then after that, a tremendous amount of guest-conducting and recording as well as commissions. With the ASCAP presidency I've had to cut back on my commissions and certainly on my conducting. It's a responsible position, and I intend to function in it as responsibly as possible, because as you and I know, the economics of our profession are very basic to enabling writers to create and get proper payment for it.

John: I remember when I got into ASCAP in 1954, they split up nine million dollars, and I think this last year they split over three hundred million. That's phenomenal.

Morton: Don't forget I've been on the ASCAP board now for, I think, some thirty years and now, of course, as president (my seventh year).

John: You have always had the reputation of being one of the finest orchestrators and arrangers of our time.

Morton: In my circumstance, I was composing before I was arranging. Arranging came very much to the forefront in my career from my compositions. I was writing my symphonic works back in the early thirties. No composer could live off that. There was no economic return—at least, not for American composers. It's only years later that an organization like ASCAP, for example, began to license symphony performances.

John: In closing what advice would you give a composer today in pursuing a life in music?

Morton: That's a big question. It depends on what kind of composer. There are very few composers who can exist economically on their compositions unless they are songwriters and are lucky out of the many people who write songs of all kinds. When I say songwriters I mean all kinds—pop, middle-of-the-road, side-of-the-road, metal, rap and so on. Of all the writers creating, a drop-in-the-bucket percentage really hit it big and can flourish economically. In other areas, for instance, symphonic composers (so-called serious or classical composers) have to do a number of things. They might have to be performers as well as composers, or teachers or all three. Or be married to somebody with a lot of money, or inherit a lot of money. But otherwise it is economically difficult. So I would say that if you are a so-called concert composer you should be qualified to teach. Either a university or some kind of job or position, or a constant employment pattern, such as doing arrangements. I mean, this is what I did. But whatever it is, you cannot exist on composition alone. There are exceptions to this, and every now and then somebody comes along . . . . But I think you will find the exceptions doing things like conducting along with composing, or else they are writing theater works of one sort or another. What I'm saying is that the composers today should be aware of computers and all the technological possibilities. This is all part of it. This is all part of our sound. I think that a composer today has to be as qualified as possible in many different facets of music, so that if one facet is temporarily not working economically, there are other means possible.

John: Morton, this has been very enlightening. I thank you very much.

FINALE

Writing music at its best is frustrating. It is even more so when one attempts to make money at it, but don't be discouraged. Just remember that in addition to their composition activities, Bach played the organ for a living, Vivaldi ran the music department at a girl's academy, and Paul Hindemith taught at American universities.

What is important is that we continue to write—and by doing so we will perfect our craft with each measure of music we scribble. There are very few of us who were fortunate enough to be endowed with the talent to create music, but talent is not enough. You'd better have a thick hide to withstand the rejections that will come your way, and be able to keep your ego in check. If you cannot tolerate this barrage, then you will be very unhappy indeed.

Today we are living in an age of instant gratification. One has computers that print out music. We touch a button, and all of a sudden we have drums, trumpets and even a violin section. It is true that these devices help the amateurs and dilettantes, but they are also helpful to a true composer or arranger. Let us not lose sight of the fact that machines do not write music, people do. In the years to come, electronics and computers will become even more sophisticated, and the temptation will be to let science do our work. Great strides have been made in computers and programs for film synchronization, for example—but again, they cannot write music. It takes a composer's imagination and skill to make the motion picture come to life. Take what you need from these devices, but don't let them take over you.

I am reminded of the time when a composer friend of mine did an entirely electronic score for a picture. Although the synthesist had all his keyboards and computers in the studio, practically everything was sequenced and loaded in advance. The projectionist put up the cue, the musician touched a button or two, and the music rolled. Everything fit well, and the music was very effective. The producer, who came to the session, nodded after every cue, which meant that he had no comments for any changes. After about an hour, he just left the stage. The composer, thinking that the producer was upset about something, asked why he was leaving. The producer replied that it wasn't any fun; there was no orchestra there, no excitement. He told the composer that the only time he felt like he was in show business was when he came to the scoring stage to listen and absorb the excitement of a studio orchestra bringing his film to life.

The excitement! That's what music is all about. There is nothing like hearing an orchestra or band tuning up and feeling the anticipation of what's to come.

I hope this book will provide some pleasant moments and maybe some instructive ones. There will be disagreements about almost everything I said, but that's okay. After all, music is a subjective art, and it is open to all kinds of interpretations.

To the lay person, what we composers do is very mysterious. "How can you think of tunes?" they ask. "Do you use a piano? What comes first, the music or the words?" and so on and so forth. Well, it *is* mysterious. Pipes are blown, strings are plucked and sawed upon and certain kinds of people sit and scrawl out funny-looking characters on paper with a pen or pencil. Then, these pipe blowers look at these funny little dots and squiggles, raise their pipes and bows and something wondrous happens.

It's called music.

GLOSSARY

STANDARD DYNAMIC LEVELS

ppp	triple piano, or pianississimo	very, very soft
pp	double piano, or pianissimo	very soft
p	piano	soft
mp	mezzo piano	half- or moderately soft
mf	mezzo forte	half- or moderately loud
f	forte	loud
ff	double forte, or fortissimo	very loud
fff	triple forte, or fortississimo	very, very loud

SPECIAL DYNAMIC EFFECTS

sfz (sf)	sforzando	loud, biting attack; sudden emphasis
sffz (sff)	sforzando	very loud, biting attack; sudden emphasis
sfp	sforzando-piano	loud, biting attack to soft
sfp ◁	sforzando-piano, crescendo	loud, biting attack, to soft; crescendoing to the next dynamic marking

ARTICULATIONS

A line under or over a note ▦ indicates it is to be given its full value.

A dot over or under a note ▦ indicates it is to be clipped short, given less than full value.

A curved line leading up to a note ▦ indicates the note is initially played a bit flat and "scooped" or "bent" upward to the true pitch. This marking can also be used between and after notes.

An inverted V over a note ▦ indicates that the note be played with a short, forceful burst.

A sideways V over a note  indicates a forceful attack of a note.

A sideways S between two notes  is called an *appoggiatura*, indicating the player is to rise quickly above the first note and back down to it before descending to the second note  This is especially effective on brass instruments.

Both a line and a sideways V above a note  indicate it is to be both attacked and given its full value.

A line descending *to* a note  is called a *rip* or a *lip gliss*. It indicates a short, undefined downward thrust terminating on the desired note. It is also used leading up to a note.

A curved line descending *from* a note  is used to indicate a *short drop* or *falloff*. A wiggly line descending *from* a note indicates a *long drop*  These two markings are often used interchangeably; to avoid confusion, the desired effect should be clearly designated.

A wiggly line *over* a note  is used to indicate a *shake*. Shakes can vary in speed, so they should be clearly labeled.

A curved line over two or more separate notes  is called a *slur*. It indicates the notes are to be played in a smooth, connected line, usually in one breath.

MUSIC PUBLISHERS

Alfred Publishing Co., Inc.
16380 Roscoe Blvd., Suite 200
Van Nuys, CA 91406

One of America's leading companies for educational music of all kinds.

CPP/Belwin, Inc.
P.O. Box 4340
Hialeah, FL 33014

Does many arrangements of current pop music in all categories. Also publishes originals in most areas.

C. L. Barnhouse Publishing Co.
P.O. Box 680
Oskaloosa, IA 52577

Primarily publishes originals and arrangements for concert band. Also has a stage-band publication program.

Bourne Co.
5 West 37th St.
New York, NY 10018

A famous pop music firm with an extensive catalog specializing in band, orchestral and choral works.

Boosey and Hawkes, Inc.
52 Cooper Square
New York, NY 10003

Publishes all kinds of serious music, chamber works and operas. Also has an educational department for band, orchestra and chorus. Maintains an extensive rental department.

Boston Music Co.
116 Boylston St.
Boston, MA 02116

Publishes primarily piano music, but also other educational works.

M. M. Cole
919 North Michigan Ave.
Chicago, IL 60611

Specializes in folios, methods and school music.

Carl Fischer
54 Cooper Square
New York, NY 10003

Publishes serious and educational instrumental works.

European-American Music
P.O. Box 850
Valley Forge, PA 19482

Publishes serious and educational instrumental works.

Galaxy Music Corp.
131 West 86th St.
New York, NY 10024

Publishes primarily serious works, opera and chamber works. Also publishes band and orchestra works for the school market.

G. Schirmer, Inc.
24 East 22nd St.
New York, NY 10010

Publishes all types of educational and serious music. Large rental department and art song catalog.

Neil A. Kjos Music Co.
4380 Jutland Dr.
San Diego, CA 92117

Publishes band and orchestra methods and has large piano program. Also publishes band, orchestral and choral works.

Kendor Music, Inc.
P.O. Box 278
Delavan, NY 14042

Large publisher of original stage band works. Also publishes works for band, orchestra and chorus.

Ludwig Music Publishing Co., Inc.
557 East 140th St.
Cleveland, OH 44110

Has an extensive catalog for band, orchestra and chorus. Also publishes methods and solos.

Queenswood Publications
11101 East Mercer Lane
Scottsdale, AZ 85259

Small but aggressive company specializing in easy band materials.

Robert King Music Co.
28 Main St.
North Easton, MA 02356

Primarily publishes music for brass ensembles and solos.

Shawnee Press, Inc.
Delaware Water Gap, PA 18327

Primarily known for their large choral catalog, they also publish works for band and orchestra.

Southern Music Co.
P.O. Box 329
San Antonio, TX 78292

Has a large catalog for band and orchestra. Also publishes smaller ensembles and solos.

Theodore Presser, Inc.
Presser Place
Bryn Mawr, PA 19010

A large company publishing all kinds of music, both educational and larger serious works. Also has an extensive rental department.

Many of the larger houses such as Warner/Chappell, Famous Music, E.B. Marks, Mills Music and so on, are currently having their publications handled by such firms as CPP/Belwin and Hal Leonard. Queries regarding submission of works are best addressed to the companies representing them. This list is not meant to be all-inclusive, but it does represent the majority of publishers today that are in the business of printing music and selling it. If you are in doubt about the specialities of any firm, your question can best be answered by the music buyers in the large retail and wholesale organizations. Among them is the J. W. Pepper Co. of Valley Forge, Pa., which has branches in many major cities in America. Although Pepper's catalogs do not list publishers, you can certainly get this information from their staff.

Many of the smaller educational firms have arrangements with larger educational firms to handle their publications. Again, the selling agents can tell you whom to submit your materials to.